The Weaponization of Trade

PERSPECTIVES

Series editor: Diane Coyle

The Weaponization of Trade

The Great Unbalancing of Politics
and Economics

Rebecca Harding
Jack Harding

Published by London Publishing Partnership
www.londonpublishingpartnership.co.uk

Published in association with
Enlightenment Economics
www.enlightenmenteconomics.com

ISBN: 978-1-907994-72-2 (pbk)

A catalogue record for this book is
available from the British Library

This book has been composed in Candara

Copy-edited and typeset by
T&T Productions Ltd, London
www.tandtproductions.com

Cover image montage by
James Shannon:
www.jshannon.com

Contents

Chapter 1

Introduction: strategic trade

> I am very disappointed in China. Our foolish past leaders have allowed them to make hundreds of billions of dollars in trade a year yet ... they do NOTHING for us with North Korea, just talk. We will no longer allow this to continue. China could easily solve this problem!
>
> — @RealDonaldTrump

International trade is about more than just economics, and not only for the US administration. Trade is about coercion and strategic influence.

Since the 2008 financial crisis, the language around trade has shifted. Before, politicians described it as a benign mechanism for promoting global economic growth. Now, their statements about trade are steeped in the rhetoric of war. Instead of global opportunities and wealth creation, politicians on both sides of the Atlantic talk about 'protection', 'security', 'national interest' and 'defence'. Former trade partners are now trade 'enemies', with 'unfair' protectionist policies against which it is natural for any politician to rail.

Through this linguistic metamorphosis, it has become apparent that trade is being used as a tool of state strategy. Trade deals have foreign policy objectives. The UK prime minister, Theresa May, and the US president, Donald Trump, have both conflated trade goals with foreign policy goals. In her Article 50 letter to the president of the European Council triggering the United Kingdom's exit from the European Union, Theresa May suggested that a trade deal could be linked to UK participation in European security arrangements. Donald Trump has explicitly linked US discussions with China to the issue of North Korea's nuclear programme.

This book argues that through this rhetorical shift, trade is being weaponized into a tool of strategic and political influence. Although 'weaponization' is an inflammatory term, in the context of trade it can be used literally. Weaponization is the transformation of a benign instrument into a means of aggression and, increasingly, we have observed states wielding trade coercively. It is redolent of Carl von Clausewitz's classic definition of war: first, as the continuation of policy by another means; and second, through the supply of arms and ammunition to strategic partners, as an indirect 'act of force to compel our enemy to do our will'.[1] In short, through language, the character of trade has changed from an *implicit* tool of coercion to the *explicit* means through which foreign policy objectives are achieved.

There are no circumstances under which this rhetorical weaponization can be seen as a good thing. The benefits of trade require a balance between economics and politics. Although trade and foreign policy have been interwoven throughout history, the belligerence of the language at present means there is a risk of trade becoming predominantly political, rather than economic. This puts at risk the economic and political gains of the period since World War II and even poses a danger of returning to the implosion of trade in the 1930s. Unless governments retreat from their current rhetoric, the scope for mistrust and retaliation will grow. Policymakers need to step back from the brink of weaponized trade policy and demonstrate that they understand their responsibilities as leaders, regulators and facilitators of trade and multilateralism.

Here we introduce the concept of 'strategic trade'. This we define as trade that is deployed not only to achieve economic and social goals domestically (its traditional role) but also to promote national interests abroad. This is achieved through integration, coercion or the targeted supply of the means for violence in regions of the world deemed to be of strategic importance without the need to engage militarily. This is crucial in an era when ineffective interventions in the twenty-first century (e.g. in Afghanistan and Iraq) have undermined the political will for direct military action.

WHAT IS STRATEGY?

At this stage we should clarify what we mean by 'strategy'. The term is often misunderstood and misappropriated, so here are four 'golden rules' for understanding strategy in the context in which it is used here.

1. Strategy has an inexorable connection with the military: the term derives from the Greek word 'strategos', meaning 'general' or 'commander', whose responsibility it was to devise and implement plans for victory in battle, war and beyond. Early strategic theory saw the concept as being limited to wartime and exclusively the domain of the general. This is evident in Clausewitz's early definition of strategy, which he saw as 'the use of engagements for the object of war'.[2] These 'engagements' are understood as a combination of single acts, including, but not limited to, the use of armed force.

2. Strategy is necessarily and inescapably linked with politics. The military theorist Basil Liddell Hart extended Clausewitz's definition of strategy by including a political dimension. He defined it as 'the art of distributing and applying military means to fulfil the ends of policy'.[3] However, in the context of the concept of strategic trade, nuclear strategist Colin Gray's definition is more helpful: strategy is 'the use made of (any) means by chosen ways in order to achieve desired political ends'.[4]

3. Strategy is fundamentally about ends (or consequences), but it is not an end in itself. Instead, it should be understood as the *ways used* to achieve policy objectives. Conventionally, this refers to military means; however, as we will argue, there seems to be an emerging trend towards the use of trade to achieve policy objectives that just fifteen years ago could have involved direct military action. As such, trade can be seen as an integral part of state strategy.

4. Strategies are a function of their cultural and social contexts. Therefore, in an era in which the political will to engage with direct military action has been undermined by domestic discontent with protracted campaigns, trade becomes an attractive strategic option. To this end, the challenge is to reconcile a chosen strategy – in this context, trade – with the will of the people; this is done through public rhetoric.

The concept of strategic trade in economic terms was developed by Paul Krugman, who, like us, argued that trade is more than just economics: it is politics too.[5] However, we broaden the concept to include the use of trade in a military context, as a means to achieve foreign policy objectives, rather than the protectionist, domestic economic objectives to which Krugman referred.

For Krugman, writing in 1986, strategic trade suggests that governments can catalyse resource reallocation to those sectors and businesses where economic rents (i.e. returns to capital and labour) are highest and protect them against foreign competition. He argued that trade was increasingly about taking national advantage of economies of scale and of the positive spillover effects (external economies) from technology and organizational learning.

Like Krugman, we also see trade as strategic. But there are two key differences between his approach and ours.

First, we define trade as a tool of both foreign and economic policy. This means that we are defining 'strategic' trade as a driver of influence in foreign policy as well as in economic terms.

Second, Krugman was writing in a period before the end of the Cold War and before the completion of the European Single Market. We argue that the free movement of capital, labour and ideas that defined the post–Cold War period has shifted the positive externalities of trade for technological and organizational purposes from the nation state to the multinational corporation, with three main effects.

- It makes the real value of trade almost impossible to measure. Services and goods trade combine in one supply chain. This increases the value of trade even if the volume of goods traded stays constant. Transactions within supply chains are hard to capture in trade statistics, and it is difficult to trace the value added and economic rents. This makes trade as a tool of national interest very difficult to gauge in economic terms. The consequence is that, just as we want to start to measure trade and trade performance nationally, trade growth itself has become unreliable – almost a Goodhart's Law of international trade flows.[6]
- It weakens the ability of domestic macroeconomic policy to capture the advantages of trade, either

through currency manipulation or through tariffs and subsidies. Companies are able to shift their operations relatively swiftly to take advantage of favourable tax regimes and subsidies. As a result, traditional policy levers can no longer deliver benefits at a domestic level.

- Proportionately, however, it increases the power of nation states and trade blocs to form aggressive policies to disadvantage another nation politically (through sanctions) without doing lasting damage to their multinational corporations. This has the effect of creating global trade 'enemies' – like China, Russia and Iran from a Western perspective – and using them in public discourse to harness war-like rhetoric.

Why look at trade strategically now?

Iconoclastic politicians have created a sense in the voting population that most people have been excluded from the benefits of globalization. Further, a wave of immigration across Europe – indeed across the world – and the perception of a greater threat from terrorism have combined to generate so-called populism that, at least in some countries, has left global liberal democracy with its own crisis of legitimacy – a democratic deficit, even.

However, at its core, the rise of populism is an acknowledgment of the power that the people hold. It is an outcome of a lack of transparency in the actions of the policy elites and it is a wake-up call to the dangers of ignoring the will of the people. In an era of social media, where every political action has a public reaction, policy needs justification. In other words, it is no longer acceptable simply to export weapons to Saudi Arabia, we now need to justify those exports – and how better than through the language of 'national interest' and 'safety and security'. This association with national interest through social media and global communications is what makes this era substantively different to previous ones.

The resultant invocation of economic nationalism can be seen as an attempt to recapture the lost territory of global leadership and to win the hearts and minds of electorates; the benefits of trade are being conflated with more nationalist agendas. In the words of one former intelligence official we interviewed as part of the research for this book, 'trade is a useful weapon in a nationalist narrative'.

We argue that this weaponization of trade has meant that politicians are using trade strategically to balance their domestic and foreign policy interests. This is clearly damaging, not just for the global economy with its reliance on multilateralism to support the principle of free trade, but also because it puts trade in a battlefield, not a boardroom. More nationalistic policies create an 'us versus them' mentality that then becomes entrenched by more aggressive political rhetoric, transforming trade from an economic tool into a political one.

Accordingly, trade can no longer remain on the peripheries of economics and international relations. The collapse of the Soviet Union changed the way that economists and strategists looked at the world. Globalization and the role of the global corporate dominated thinking, alongside a narrow narrative on the mutual benefits of multilateral trade. Globalization was seen in terms of cross-border technology transfer and the free movement of labour and capital. As such, trade was a function of corporate strategy rather than economic policy, and up to 2014, export-led growth and globalization became the mantras of politicians and business leaders alike. However, those leaders failed to consider the international relations consequences of their interpretation of the global triumph of liberal democracy and economics.

Simultaneously, a new body of literature on conflict emerged. There was a sense that 'old' large-scale wars, which were a function of the military–industrial complex of the Cold War era and before, had given way to 'new' or 'fourth-generation' conflicts characterized by small-scale local conflicts, insurgency and counterinsurgency. Fourth-generation wars were seen as a function of the contradictory political pressures of globalization; states had lost their 'monopoly on the use of armed violence'[7] as non-state actors operating among the people began to dominate conflicts. For the nation states involved, protracted and relatively unsuccessful military campaigns

– most recently in Afghanistan and Iraq – have eroded the public and political will for this type of multilateral engagement.

So, if the character of both war and globalization has changed, how do nation states wield the same global influence? We are witnessing a 'political' phase of globalization in which trade becomes an instrument of foreign policy. The appeal of this is that the *direct* military risks are one step removed, allowing states to influence outcomes *indirectly* without 'boots on the ground'. A weaponized narrative provides the vehicle for communicating and justifying this strategy to the public.

WHY IMPROVEMENTS IN DATA ENABLE THIS ANALYSIS

In this book we use a database with statistics on trade flows for 200 countries and 12,800 products. Official trade statistics often do not match bilateral flows of imports and exports: for example, imports to the United Kingdom from Germany should equal exports from Germany to the United Kingdom. In this example, the flows differ but not by much, so we take a simple average of the two numbers, both by sector and in the aggregate.

Often, though, the differences are much bigger. In these cases we take one of two routes.

1. If the difference is between 5% and 49%, we use statistical techniques to assess which country has the most reliable data and take an average of the two flows weighted more heavily towards the statistics of the more reliable country.

2. If the difference is bigger, or one country does not report the statistics, we take the data from the best reporting country.

This is a standard technique used by organizations such as the OECD and the World Trade Organization. We apply it to all countries and sectors (over one billion data points at any one point in time) using big-data techniques. It means that our database has far fewer gaps in it than alternatives because many countries, in the Middle East and Africa for example, do not report trade or do so infrequently. We use data from more reliable countries: Germany's imports data to measure Saudi Arabia's exports to Germany, for example.

Our big-data approach is particularly helpful for exploring strategic trade products such as arms and dual-use goods, which are largely hidden in other databases.

The database, which draws on data from the United Nations Comtrade Database and (for services) the UN, OECD and Eurostat, is publicly available through Equant Analytics.

The structure of the book

This book draws on multiple disciplines and is an attempt to pull together areas of politics, trade and foreign policy in a way that illustrates the challenges of the next few years.

Chapter 2 explores how the conflation of power, nationalism and trade lends populism a more militaristic agenda. As such, trade's utility is often reduced to black and white choices: to promote a national agenda or to be internationalist. However, the risk of such binary, reductionist, thinking is that trade and security become explicitly linked through political rhetoric. Where pre-war Imperialism had relatively few tools to communicate to a mass audience, modern government has round-the-clock social, digital, online and orthodox global media to use as communication vehicles. This has created the febrile 'fake news' and 'post fact' political environment that is increasingly generating a 'weaponized narrative'.[8] This narrative is ever more nationalistic, increasingly dangerous, and ultimately self-defeating. The chapter looks at why trade has been weaponized. It explores populism and nationalism in the context of both weaponized language and the need for politicians to restore democratic legitimacy.

Chapter 3 develops the concept of strategic trade as the starting point of the political phase of globalization. We distinguish between internationalism, which is defined by its discrete and largely bilateral economic or political relationships, and globalization, which is characterized by systemic international relationships that alter the political, economic, social and international relations paradigms. Up to 1990 and the end of the Cold War, the nation state had clear influence, both economically and militarily: economically through allocation of capital and labour according to national interest, and militarily through so-called industrial wars. However, the chapter notes that as globalization gathered pace during the

1990s and beyond – and the world became 'flatter'[9] and more 'weightless',[10] both economically and militarily – national interest and the benefits of multilateralism became harder to explain to voters. This contributed to the populist backlash we have witnessed since 2014. To reassert their domestic and international influence, 'nation states', or more specifically, their politicians, have sought to popularize national interest. Trade wars have therefore become a means to achieving national strategic objectives.

Chapter 4 looks at the role of strategic trade in underpinning power both nationally and abroad and how it transcends the traditional soft–hard power dichotomy. It argues that countries with a strong economic presence through trade – such as Germany, China and indeed Japan – have built global power through economic means. Their power is 'soft' in that they dominate global trade flows and have a trade surplus that increases the dependency of deficit nations. China's soft power is backed by a strong military; thus its powers of coercion are greater than those of Germany. The United States and the United Kingdom, in contrast, present their 'hard powers' before their soft power. The effective balancing of the two widens the 'strategic choice' available to a nation. While the United States competes with China as the world's largest trading nation, it uses its military strength, rather than its economic strength, to coerce.

The chapter suggests that we are at a historical juncture in the development of hard and soft power as a means of achieving strategic objectives. With soft power comes responsibility and, to this point, America has seen its responsibility as the global policeman to ensure that its doctrine of liberal democracy is spread as widely as possible. It appeared to have been successful during the second era of globalization but, by pursuing its own national objectives, especially in the Middle East, it has sown the seeds of the challenges it now faces. The 'Make America Great' response regards the post-war years as having been 'unfair' in their treatment of US interests and therefore seeks to recalibrate trade back in their favour.

Chapter 5 looks at the amount of trade in the world that is unexplained at any one point in time. It then examines trends in the global arms trade and in the trade of dual-use goods (goods with both civilian and military applications). There is evidence that arms and dual-use goods trade clearly reflects the strategic interests of a state. By definition, dual-use goods can be used for civilian and military purposes. For example, a shipment of electronic devices to Estonia may be for household consumption, but it may equally be used to bolster Europe's cyber defences. That is, in the words of one interviewee for this book, 'trade in goods with dual-use purpose is used by individuals with no formal military training to fight wars against an unknown and unquantifiable enemy'. Because of this, we take the broadest possible definition of dual-use goods to illustrate both the strength of the correlation between growth in this trade and gross domestic product (GDP), and as a proxy for the strategic intent of a nation state.

Chapter 6 looks at the consequences in relation to modern warfare: political conflict, violence or insurgency at a localized level. This type of conflict bears all the hall-marks of the second phase of globalization in terms of the use of new technologies, myriad international con-nections and 'a revolution in the social relations of war-fare'.[11] The chapter demonstrates that a country with a low GDP per capita is nearly four times more likely to experience political instability than a country with high GDP. Moreover, a country whose arms imports increased by more than 40% over the period from 1989 to 2015 is nearly five times more likely to experience political insta-bility than a country with lower arms trade growth.

This has significant consequences. First, trade in arms represents the chosen means for more developed nations to direct proxy wars. Second, the use of trade as a means of warfare is becoming more explicit. Third, in the politicized stage of globalization, and since NATO's withdrawal from Afghanistan, the 'arm's-length' and trade-based approach to conflict is likely to increase. We see Saudi Arabia's arms trade with the United Kingdom and the United States and the war in Yemen as evidence of the destructive power of this latest phase.

Chapter 7 is an overview of some of the policy implications. We argue that the current rhetoric is undermining the global institutions that were constructed after World War II to ensure peace and economic stability. The responsibility will necessarily fall on regulators to rebalance the politics and the economics of trade and this chapter argues that there should be no retreat from free trade and multilateralism if global stability is to be maintained.

Chapter 8 argues that the concept of strategic trade helps us to understand why trade has been weaponized and how it is being used as a means to promote national interests, in both foreign policy and economic terms. Indeed, we conclude that since 2014, the economics and the politics of international trade have both been harnessed to a nationalist rhetoric driven by the dual interests of restoring the democratic legitimacy of Western nation states and providing a means to an end where overt military means have failed.

Interpreting trade in this way points to its potential as a tool for restoring multilateral and consensus-based routes to strategic influence. Accordingly, the chapter discusses the role of global leadership and soft power in helping to ensure that the world does not take a dangerous turn at this historical crossroads. It concludes with an analysis of trade finance, regulation and compliance policies that would begin to tip the balance back towards trade's positive economic role.

Trade is more than an economic concept; and trade wars are not just protectionism. Strategic trade is one way in which countries can build their influence and power globally, and trade can be used in part as a substitute for direct military intervention. The weaponized trade rhetoric has correctly identified this strategic role and the constant balance between economics and politics in trade policy.

But the weaponization is risky because it threatens the fabric of both the global economy and national economies. Companies need free trade rather than protectionism in the interests not just of jobs and wealth creation but also of social gains such as cultural exchange, foreign travel and reciprocal employment abroad.

Current rhetoric is putting at risk many trade and political relationships in Europe, in the United States and throughout the world. Policymakers must address both the current political instabilities and the strategic role for trade. One theme emerged consistently in our interviews: the need for politicians to take some responsibility for the rise of populism. At this moment of crisis, weaponized language has the potential to do lasting damage.

Perhaps Brexit and Trump will represent a catharsis, but the responsibility now lies with politicians to explain to their publics why globalization is important. It is the language that poses the risk, not the awareness of the national interest embodied in strategic trade. Trade policies should recognize the economic issues identified by Paul Krugman. Perhaps if the strategic aspects of trade were better understood and articulated, those who speak in weaponized terms about trade would begin to show due humility.

Chapter 2

The populist context

Trade, strategic influence and nationalism

The continuum on which countries and businesses interact with each other internationally is commonly referred to as globalization. This continuum is now entering a new phase that is conceptually different. It is overtly political, focused on national interests, and is arguably the product of a wave of populism and anti-globalization sentiment. The result is that trade has itself become a means to achieving the objectives of the nation state, in foreign policy, security and economic terms.

Where better to look for evidence of this than to Donald Trump. After his first meeting with Xi Jinping, on 11 April 2017, Trump tweeted: 'I explained to the President of China that a trade deal with the US will be far better for them if they solve the North Korean problem!' In other words, Trump's view of the utility of trade had a strong political undercurrent. Accordingly, Mike Pence, the US vice president, embarked on a ten-day tour of

Asia to talk to America's allies in the region, including South Korea and Japan, with whom it runs big (read problematic) trade surpluses and whose buy-in and support the United States would need in the event of any military engagement with North Korea.

This is not just the domain of the United States of course. Only a week before that Trump tweet, in her speech launching the Article 50 process to take the United Kingdom out of the European Union (EU), Theresa May linked Brexit trade negotiations with Britain's continued role in EU intelligence and security. This irritated European negotiators, but more seriously it also conflated the relationship between trade and military power in the same way that the Brexit campaign itself had conflated immigration and terrorism.

In this chapter we explore the concept of populism and why an understanding of strategic trade will help shed light on the future direction that the world may take. There is no doubting that this is a serious moment; as Martin Wolf argues, 'We live in the world the US made. Now it is unmaking it. We cannot ignore that grim reality.'[12] Interviewees for this book were also similarly concerned about the future. As a senior trade and sanctions lawyer argued:

> It is a dangerous time and we will see a lasting legacy from what is happening now. There is a dialectic that we are seeing where the forces of globalization driven through

technology have advantaged some in terms of social mobility and disadvantaged others. We are living in a world of real-time politics where nobody has the answers.

Globalization itself helps explain why we are at this point. Its progress has created the uncertainties we see now. It is not that free trade and global movements of capital and labour are not intuitively a good thing, it is that their benefits are not obvious to the general population, who see a lack of economic improvement in their own lives, distancing the electorate from politics. The result is populism, or at the very least direct public scrutiny of the democratic legitimacy of international institutions, globalization and its accompanying free movement of labour (immigration and the conflation with terrorism) and of capital (perceived inequalities).

Trade is the logical route to connect the national economic interest with the national strategic interest. Globalization is both politicized and nationalized at the same time, and nowhere has this been better captured than in the 'Buy American, Hire American' executive order signed by Donald Trump in April 2017[13] or the United Kingdom's 'Exporting is Great' campaign.[14] Trade policy immediately becomes a tool to protect domestic interests and to further strategic interests abroad. In short, it gives politicians a means of reconnecting with their electorates when traditional

21

economic and foreign policy mantras have failed. It also, intentionally or otherwise, bolsters nationalist sentiments.

This chapter describes the origins and the features of populism that have led to the political phase of globalization that is now unfolding. Underpinning it are the uncertainties that globalization has produced in terms of uneven economic benefits, the rise of migration, and, in the mind of the popular media at least, its conflation with a lack of domestic job security and the perceived rise in the frequency of indiscriminate terror attacks. In an atmosphere of global uncertainty, individuals feel that they do not have control of their own destinies. Populism is an attempt by the voting public to regain control at the ballot box: through Brexit in the United Kingdom and through the election of President Trump in the United States, for example. The chapter concludes that the increased use of weaponized language is a logical consequence of this process: trade arrangements or multilateral agreements are 'unfair', there are national interests to 'defend' and jobs and people to 'protect'. The rhetoric fills a void that has been left by the impotence of orthodox economic and foreign policy tools to resolve domestic issues or promote strategic influence. The result of all this is the effective creation of an enemy against which a nation can combine to fight.

Globalization: the origins of populism and weaponized language

Populism is a by-product of globalization. Technological change and the free movement of people and capital were regarded as universally positive. According to former BT chairman Ben Verwaayen, as he heralded the growing global mobility of labour in 2005:

> It takes a dog, a chair and a computer to be part of the global workforce. The dog to wake you up, the chair to sit down on, and the computer to connect you to the rest of the world.

The challenge for policymakers was to raise skills to compete with highly trained and motivated young graduates in emerging economies, to see the world as a vehicle for achieving dreams, and to innovate in order to 'get ahead'. Liverpool's port was no longer competing with Southampton or Felixstowe: it was competing with Hamburg, Dubai ... even Singapore.

It should come as little surprise that the advantages of this world order have been hard to explain to people on the outside; in fact, on both sides of the Atlantic, the enthusiasm for globalization has reversed. Political rhetoric has shifted to equate 'uncertainty' and 'fear' with globalization over the past couple of years. This rise of populism has strong anti-immigration tendencies, where a lack of national and personal security is tied to a lack of economic security. This is seen as the result of globalization and the consequent threat to employment from 'others' outside of a domestic labour market. Technology and mass migration (including that of refugees) have altered the expectations of national labour markets and welfare systems.

It is the perceived link, however misguided, between immigration, lack of income growth and terrorism that has allowed populism to gain ground.

Nationalist sentiments were particularly evident in Britain in June 2016 when the Brexit referendum was held. Frustrations rose over the perception that immigration was leading to job losses and allowing terrorists into the country, while for many there was a sense of anger at their perceived lack of political power, which they associated with the flawed democratic legitimacy of the EU. With a majority of 52% to 48%, the British public voted to leave.

Four major terrorist incidents in France meant that no one blinked when presidential candidate Marine Le Pen suggested during the Easter weekend in 2017, ahead of the run-up to first-round voting in the French presidential election,[15] that she would ban 'all legal immigration' to stop a 'mad, uncontrolled situation' were she to be elected. In the end, Emmanuel Macron was elected as president, prompting a wave of commentary arguing that populism was on the wane in Europe. But this may have been premature, given that 25% of the electorate abstained and a further 9% spoiled their ballot papers.

Meanwhile, in Germany, the Alternative für Deutschland (AfD) party has morphed from offering an academic critique of the country's adoption of the euro as its currency to being a full-blown anti-immigration party. The fact that it gained 12.6% of the vote in Germany's recent election demonstrates the frustration that is felt with the traditional parties in Germany. However, it will not be in government – only in the parliament – and, as one young German voter added, 'we know a thing or two about extremism in Germany and we know we could have a lot of power at the moment – that worries us'. This sense of growing global responsibility in Germany was evident from the interviews we conducted. A former diplomat added:

> We don't like the word leadership. We have had a *Führer* and don't want that again. But we understand that we can't sit back anymore.

The rise of populism is well-trodden ground – many have tried to explain it but most of the explanations feel like a reaffirmation of the old problems. For example, in his book *The Road to Somewhere*, David Goodhart argues that the 'anywheres' (the middle-class and well-educated global elite, constituting about 25% of the United

Kingdom's population) dominate political discourse and economic success.[16] As a result of their success and their internationalism, he argues, the 'somewheres', who are rooted in a geographical (i.e. national or local) identity, feel excluded and detached from any sense of control over their economic or political identity. The problem, of course, is that any solution put forward by a 'Remoaner'[17] or someone from the global elite just seems patronizing. So Goodhart and others just describe the problem and provide no solutions, for fear of sounding 'undemocratic'. Andrew Marr, in his robust critique of Goodhart's book, argues that it was a series of mistakes by British governments from the 1980s onwards, including the Iraq War in 2003, that caused the disconnect.[18] For example, the then prime minister's prioritization of strategic interests abroad and disregard for public opinion detracted from the focus on what were felt to be important domestic issues. Oil and the special relationship with the United States took precedence over voter concerns.

Nevertheless, there is a general consensus that the global populism that has been evident over the past two years or so is creating both turbulence and a more 'dangerous' era ahead. This danger does not come from public frustration with the legitimacy of political processes as built into a populist movement. Rather, it comes from the use of that populism to reassert the nationalist strategies of the state: that is, populism has provided a convenient platform from which to recalibrate state strategy, both militarily and economically.

What is globalization?

The evolution of 'globalization' is, again, well-trodden ground and will be referred to again in subsequent chapters. It is nevertheless helpful to look at how it has progressed to see where the next phase will lead us.

We view the process of internationalism as a continuum. Economic, social and political interaction predate modernity and, as a result, any attempt to classify phases is fraught with difficulty, not least because it encourages commentators, including us, to talk in terms of eras 'ending' or as no longer being relevant, if indeed they ever started.[19]

However, grouping periods of time into phases is a convenient tool and an irresistible mechanism for presenting stylized facts. Internationalism is trade and foreign relations across borders.[20] Globalization represented a paradigm shift: international activity and interactions changed the way in which politics, economics and society operated domestically. Because we are looking at this process in both economic and foreign policy terms, we are loosely grouping globalization into four periods, starting with the transition to modernity and the nation state.

Imperialism and empire (1800–1945)

Like Baldwin's 'old' globalization[21] we see this as being driven by a process of rapid technological change and by the quest for new markets and territories abroad. This means that, far from being a period of relative stability, as Baldwin suggests, it is a period of power games and conflict centred around trade. The role of trade in creating power was central, because economics and politics are connected through its weapons: tariffs, exchange controls, sanctions and capital investment, to name a few.[22] The rise of the nation state during this period was the consequence of the modernity that came from the process of industrialization and technological change.[23] Hirschman's seminal *National Power and the Structure of Foreign Trade*, written in 1945, points out that the pursuit of influence can be focused as much on the *means* of creating power (e.g. through trade) as on the *ends* of power and national interest itself.[24]

The Cold War (1945–90)

Unlike Baldwin, we have separated out the Cold War period from the period of globalization up to the end of World War II. The Cold War period is commonly, and perhaps erroneously, associated in the economics literature with the dominance of the nation state. However, the nation state evolved during the earlier phase, as Hirschman points out, to support trade. So, the main distinction between the second period and the pre-war period is that in the second, nation states built vast military–industrial complexes. In other words, the literature confuses the nation state with its military–industrial complex capable of fighting large-scale, industrial – even nuclear – wars. Although supranational organizations were present, bilateral relationships dominated both international relations and trade. In Hirschman's terms, this era represents trade dominated by mercantilism. Trade is an instrument of power because more of it implies greater wealth and, hence, influence. Because this wealth through trade is at the expense of the wealth of another nation, protectionist brinkmanship ran in parallel to the 'war of nerves'[25] that was endemic to the Cold War.

'New' globalization (1990–2014)

Following the collapse of the Soviet Union, the bipolar world order came to an end, leading to greater multipolarity in international relations. This forced a total reevaluation of how states approached economic and foreign policy. The focus was on greater connectivity during the 1990s, the rise of 'Western liberalism'[26] and 'new threats' like small wars, insurgencies and counter-insurgencies such as those identified by Mary Kaldor.[27] 'New' globalization is the term used by Baldwin to describe the shift in trade power to emerging nations through information and communications technologies and free movement of capital and labour. This concept is discussed in more detail in subsequent chapters but what is important here is that while authors and commentators were claiming the 'end of history',[28] a new multipolar, multilateral order was also emerging. It was not necessarily driven through nation states but it affected national interest nevertheless.

Political globalization (2013/14 onwards)

It may seem premature to declare a new era after such a short period of time, but there are patterns of economic nationalism and foreign policy isolationism that are already evident. There is something different about this era, in that neither economic nor military policies, as they have evolved through globalization, appear to be serving the national strategic interests as well as they did. In the wake of the global financial crisis the orthodox tools of economic management have been ineffectual in stimulating sustained economic growth. Further, protracted military interventions, most notably in Afghanistan and Iraq, have not yielded the level of success expected by policymakers. This, coupled with public discontent over the efficacy of military interventions, has seriously undermined the political will for direct military engagement with 'boots on the ground'. A case in point here is the decision not to intervene in

Syria in 2013 following chemical weapons attacks in Ghouta – an attack that had flagrantly crossed Barack Obama's so-called red line. We contend that trade offers politicians another means of influence in an era where the efficacy of interventions and the public and political will for action have weakened while imperatives for economic growth have strengthened. The evidence that trade is used strategically is presented later in this book, but the fact that trade seems to be used as a weapon of war draws worrying parallels with the first phase of globalization highlighted above.

Weaponized language, trade and politics

In most of the phases of globalization there are parallels between game theory, trade and military strategy. The first phase was characterized by a distinct 'you lose, I win' approach as nation states modernized. The second, the Cold War phase, applied game theory (particularly the concept of the zero-sum game) to nuclear strategy and allowed for mercantilist approaches to trade through protectionism. During the third phase, as technology allowed information to flow freely, everyone gained from free trade and multilateralism in economic terms.

The fourth phase described above looks to be a rhetorical recalibration of the third phase, away from multilateralism and back to bilateralism, with trade as the chosen means by which to achieve policy objectives. In other words, trade is being weaponized on two levels. The first is as an instrument of state strategy and foreign policy – and this constitutes the framework for the rest of this book. The second is as part of a weaponized language around trade and foreign policy – as a reflection of economic nationalism, and nationalism more generally. For example, in the twenty years before the financial crisis and immediately after it, commentators spoke enthusiastically about the growth of south–south trade. There were investment opportunities, there was untold wealth in emerging markets, technology meant that we would share ideas and create a borderless world, and even that fully fledged war would be a thing of the past. We talked about performance, integration and global citizenship with 'opportunities for all'.

In the last two years all this has changed. Anti-globalization rhetoric is no longer the domain of a bunch of student radicals sitting outside G20 summits. It is mainstream, and it is the daily language of the most important politicians in the world. In January 2017 the front cover headline of The Economist was 'In retreat: global companies in the era of protectionism'.[29] Words associated with war are now commonplace in connection with trade: trade wars, currency wars, protection, security, defence, campaign and, most importantly, national interest. And as if to reinforce the point, the US administration is threatening the imposition of tariffs on EU steel imports on 'national security' grounds, while, following the test of a hydrogen bomb by North Korea, Donald Trump warned that the United States 'is considering, in addition to other options, stopping all trade with any country doing business with North Korea'.[30]

Some of this simply reflects the fact that trade growth itself has been disappointing since the financial crisis. Global trade, between the 1990s and the financial crisis, grew at roughly twice the rate of GDP. This made export-led growth *implicitly* the rallying cry for the nation within the global sphere of economic influence.

As figure 1 shows, trade has not grown at twice the rate of GDP since 2010, and, in fact, this is a somewhat mythical figure anyway: between 1999 and 2008 real output growth globally grew by 4.2% while trade volume growth grew by 6.6%.[31] Nevertheless, trade is known to be strongly associated with GDP growth. Our own calculations suggest that the correlation between trade growth and GDP growth is a very strong 95%. In other words, the power of trade can be invoked as an economic wake-up call to the electorate because it harks back to a previous era of greatness and a future era of influence.

This approach has developed intrinsic policy appeal because political rhetoric is not just driven by a desire to increase democratic legitimacy in the electorate. Because trade is now growing at only 80% of the rate of GDP, economists, business leaders and governments alike are looking to understand the reasons why.

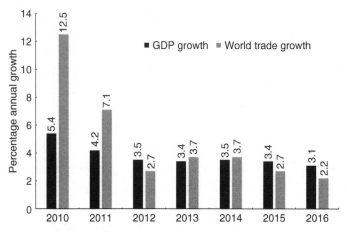

Figure 1. Real GDP versus trade volume growth since the financial crisis. *Source*: IMF, 2017.

The obvious cause of this pattern is the process of globalization itself: trade is falling back because it is not nations that trade with each other, but businesses. The global corporate has shortened its supply chains, located to maximize performance as well as product-ivity, rendering old, country-based, economic models of comparative advantage entirely redundant. Digitization and new working practices, including the increased ser-vice component of manufacturing, have promoted the 'dog, chair and computer' model of globalization.

The result is that, as the McKinsey Global Institute estimates, the trade link to GDP is stronger in countries that have higher technology components; indeed, tech-nology adds between 15% and 25% in value terms every year.[32] The McKinsey analysis was based on 2012 data and we have since seen visibly flatter world trade growth in nominal value terms for both goods and services (figure 2).

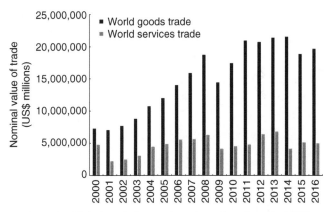

Figure 2. Global trade in goods and services (nominal US$ values, 2000–2016). *Source*: Equant Analytics, 2017.

But the point remains that technology is now an integral part of the process of global trade. Indeed, trade is so dominated by technology that the phrase 'manufacturing as a service' is commonplace: alongside the supply of goods comes the supply of a service as well. This development is both trade's driver and its downfall: it speeds up the growth of global corporates but alongside that it also accelerates the logical outcome of globalization, which is localization on cost, efficiency and effectiveness grounds. So instead of specialization and zero-sum games, in business terms globalization means regionalization and competitiveness.

Concluding remarks

All of this is problematic for state strategy and, in a sense, is at the heart of the current policy challenge. At an economic level, the third phase of globalization removed the power to regulate trade (directly through tariffs or indirectly through non-tariff barriers like regulation). As a result, governments in the political phase find themselves without adequate control over their trade or current account deficits, and hence they have only limited influence over how the economy grows. Combined with the fact that central banks are largely independent – and have since the financial crisis set monetary policy to provide liquidity for growth – this has meant that governments have effectively lost control of the real levers of macroeconomic policy: to central banks and global capital flows on the one hand and to the largesse of global corporates on the other. Appealing to the public's anti-globalization and anti-corporate sentiments through trade and nationalism could simply be seen as a strategic manoeuvre by governments to reestablish their own power.

Old politics says 'it's the economy stupid', and that captures the hearts and minds of a country's electorate. Populist politics is more subtle: 'it's *our* economy stupid' means that the economic interests of the nation are paramount. The individual is at once a citizen of that nation and empowered by the economic nationalism that results. Whoever heard of public outrage at another country's trade surplus? Yet this seems to be the sentiment expressed by the current US administration. Trade with the world is the way to both secure jobs at home and feel pride in a nation's global status without feeling the threat of globalization. And mixing trade deals rhetorically with, for example, greater expenditure on NATO, the threat from North Korea or the maintenance of European security brings trade, power and the nation back together and back to the heart of the nationalism they evoke.

Populism appears to be both a cause and an effect of the rise of economic nationalism and the weaponized language that is being used to promote national interests through trade. The policy response to uncertainty and, indeed, fear has been aimed at recalibrating the domestic influence of politics. This is a dangerous road: weaponized language creates enemies, and since trade is a traditional tool of grand strategy, it becomes a weapon. The warning to politicians, therefore, is to handle trade with care – to step back from the current rhetoric, which is too dangerous to be used loosely.

The remainder of this book draws on data, literature, documentary evidence and twenty interviews with senior trade negotiators, diplomats, policymakers and financiers from the United Kingdom, Germany and France to analyse the weaponization of trade (indeed trade wars) as a means of furthering strategic influence. We believe this is an important interpretation of events that will help further understanding both of what is at stake and of what might still be achieved. In the words of one French advocate with whom we spoke:

> For centuries, politicians had to win real wars to keep the 'enemy' in check. Now they have to do something else – so they are turning to trade and this weaponizes both economic and foreign policy.

Chapter 3

From economic nationalism to trade wars

The discussion so far has highlighted the importance of the link between trade and power, or, more specifically, the role of strategic trade in achieving a nation's foreign policy objectives.

This approach is justified for two reasons. First, there is a phase of globalization that is now unfolding that has taken trade from its simple economic dimension into the dimension of foreign policy because of recent events: Brexit and the election of President Trump in particular. Second, a 'weaponized' trade-based narrative that sees trade partners as 'enemies' is also evident as a product of economic nationalism. Trade deals are now in the 'national interest' but have been linked by policymakers on both sides of the Atlantic to military and security issues.

This is a departure from the conventional view of trade. It is a revival of the link between foreign trade and power discussed by Albert Hirschman in the context of the build-up to World War II. Similarly, Ronald Findlay and Kevin O'Rourke addressed this concept in their analysis of interregional trade through history and its interface with economic and political power. This connection has always been important: evidence presented in subsequent chapters suggests that the link between trade and power has been apparent throughout the 'new' globalization era from the end of the Cold War up to 2014. However, what is different now is the rhetorical shift: from economic nationalist language to weaponized language. The logical consequence is that an ensuing 'war' will be 'fought' through trade. This has consequences both for how we define a trade war and for how we integrate the role of trade into a definition of war that captures its strategic purpose both economically and in terms of influence.

The goal of this chapter is to develop the concept of strategic trade as the starting point of the political phase of globalization. To do this we focus first on economic nationalism and current rhetoric in the United States and the United Kingdom in order to capture the contextual tensions surrounding trade's new role. From this starting point we go on to look at the concept of a 'trade war' in order to establish a working definition of war that applies equally to trade and to armed conflict. This provides the backdrop to the evidence on strategic trade that is presented in subsequent chapters.

'Trade war': economic nationalism and aggressive rhetoric

What do we understand by the term 'trade war'? In a purely economic sense the term refers to protectionism, and it can therefore be seen as an appealing tool to support economic nationalism through the protection of domestic industries. The International Monetary Fund (IMF), the World Trade Organization (WTO) and the EU regard protectionism as a barrier to economic growth and economic development through free trade. For example, in 2016 the WTO reported the highest monthly average increase in the number of protectionist measures by its members since 2011, with 154 restrictive measures being introduced.[33] Trade did decline in nominal value terms by approximately 15% between 2015 and 2016, but this was as much a function of the collapse of commodity prices as it was of trade restrictions: over the same period there were 132 measures facilitating world trade, and the trade protectionist measures that were introduced were very targeted at specific sectors by specific countries. In other words, trade protectionism has until recently not had much of an impact on trade; trade wars in the economic sense are arguably limited in scope and impact.

Rhetorical trade wars, in contrast, are a political rallying cry. However, the weaponized language both creates an enemy in the public's eye and, more importantly, overly politicizes trade. In Hirschman's words, it leads to the 'war of nerves' that is endemic to the creation of influence and power. In other words, the rhetoric foments 'mind games' that can best be interpreted through game theory, with nationalism and internationalism as the strategic choices between two or more participants.

Is this new? The short answer is no, but the mechanisms have changed. In 1945 Hirschman argued that trade creates winners and losers, or, in his words, relations of dependency and domination out of 'mutually beneficial' trade.[34] He stated that the dominant country will, over time, begin to seek power through trade, not just over weaker nations but also with stronger nations. In his view, that process leads to the creation of political, as well as economic, power. The central idea is that as the dominant power builds, its attention is diverted from the weaker nation, and that this process ultimately plants the seeds of its own destruction as the weaker power looks elsewhere for support. The dominant power becomes focused on power in and for itself, and this one important factor helps to explain the rise of imperialism among other things.[35] In other words, because the nation state controls the economic institutions of trade *and* has a monopoly on the use of violence in the national (economic) interest, power and trade cannot be separated.[36]

What is war?

Given the inextricable link between trade, power, politics and coercion, the term 'trade war' is applicable beyond its limited use in economics. This necessarily requires an exploration of what war *is* and what it *is not*.

Numerous definitions of war exist, from the very vague, 'a violent contact of distinct but similar entities',[37] to the overly specific, 'at least 1,000 battle-related deaths per year'.[38] However, neither of these definitions is particularly satisfactory. The first could also apply to a car crash, while the second would, for example, exclude the 1982 Falklands War, which saw 907 casualties.

In fact, most attempts at providing a definition of war usually fall short of that supplied by the Prussian general Carl von Clausewitz in his nineteenth-century work *On War*. He defines war in several ways: as 'a duel on a larger scale', as 'an act of force to compel our enemy to do our will' and, of course, as the famous and widely quoted 'continuation of policy by other means'. Clausewitz also identifies a number of essential components that necessarily comprise a war. Most notably: it must be political; it must be violent; and it must be instrumental, i.e. the objective must be change or coercion. Further, he writes that any theory of war must take into account the role of the people, the military and the government, and the interconnected nature of the relationship between all three.

The acuity of thought demonstrated by Clausewitz is evidenced by the fact that nearly 200 years later we still do not have a better definition of war – and we will not attempt to improve upon the definition here either. Rather, we would like to introduce our own definition as a summary of Clausewitz's principal arguments. With an added temporal dimension, we define war as 'sustained violent action, directed by politics, between two or more armed actors with the objective of imposing their will'.

Trade wars

How far, then, does our concept of a 'trade war' adhere to this definition of conventional warfare? Although we have taken some liberties in our comparison between conventional warfare and 'trade wars', the parallels between the two are nonetheless intriguing and revelatory.

Clearly, trade is as much about politics as it is about economics. It can be wielded by a state as an instrument of policy with the objective, in some circumstances, of bending other states to its will. For example, if it so wished, China could cut off trade ties with North Korea if it continues to develop its nuclear weapons programme.

Similarly, trade can be used to prop up regimes or fuel insurgencies. A case in point here would be Russia's exports to Syria in support of Bashar al-Assad or the corresponding supply of arms to Saudi Arabia by the United Kingdom and the United States in a bid to influence outcomes to their respective benefits. These are discussed in later chapters in more detail.

Further, given how the language around trade has been 'weaponized', we are also seeing evidence of states creating a perception among the general population that trade partners are 'enemies'. Not only does this potentially create two opposing sides, but it is also clearly an attempt at legitimizing the action taken with the 'emotions and passions' of the people.

Where our view of trade wars hits a slight obstacle is on the element of violence. Trade in itself is not violent, and we would not claim the contrary. As such, we cannot argue that trade wars are wars in the definitional sense. However, trade in certain sectors – most obviously arms – can supply the means for violence in a target state or region. This allows the exporting states to protect their strategic interests through the provision of weaponry, thereby influencing the outcome of the conflict without direct military engagement. Thus, it can be *indirectly* violent or, put simply, aggressive in character. In this sense, to borrow British military strategist Basil Liddell Hart's theory, trade is an effective component of the 'indirect approach'.

So trade has the potential to adhere to many of the elements included in a traditional definition of war: it can be political, coercive and instrumental. Further, and more recently, we have seen evidence of political elites attempting to reconcile their actions with the general population. Although trade is not necessarily violent, it can be carried out with the intention of fuelling violence. The danger now, given the increased use of weaponized language around trade, is escalation.

The context of economic nationalism

The reason for the phrase 'trade wars' becoming commonplace is linked to the liberal use of the phrase 'zero sum' in order to justify increasing economic nationalism. In the words of one interviewee, 'the phrase "win–win" has been replaced by "zero sum"'. The phrase is now being used loosely to describe the actions of another country as 'unfair', and hence to justify some kind of retaliation, such as border taxes, tariffs or non-tariff barriers.

Since President Trump's inauguration, trade discourse, particularly through social media, has been strewn with implicit references to trade wars: China, for example, has an 'unfair' surplus with the United States, and while the US president in the end did not brand the Chinese government as 'currency manipulators', he did set a 100-day deadline for Chinese and US negotiators to strike a fairer deal for the United States. This reached its climax with Steve Bannon's statement before he left the White House that, 'we're at economic war with China'. Similarly, Germany has been described as 'bad, very bad' because of its trade surplus with the United States, particularly in terms of its exports of cars, which have been described as 'terrible'. Even Christine Lagarde of the IMF has warned that the belligerent language is 'sowing the seeds' of a trade war through protectionism that is not helpful for the world economy, emerging markets or, indeed, the world's exporting businesses.

One possible reason for Lagarde taking this view is because the rhetoric creates a common 'enemy', which then justifies protectionism. For example, Wilbur Ross, who has been charged with developing and articulating US trade policy, sees the United States as less protectionist than its Japanese, European and Chinese counterparts:

> We also have trade deficits with all three of those places. So they talk free trade. But in fact what they practise is protectionism. And every time we do anything to defend ourselves, even against the puny obligations that they have, they call that protectionism. It's rubbish.[39]

However, Martin Wolf cogently argues that, in fact, it is 'what Mr Ross says that is rubbish'.[40] There is little chance of the US trade deficit being closed through protectionism, he argues. This is because 'exports are just another way of supplying imports': that is, if taxes on imports make a country import less, then it is very likely that it will also export less. In short:

> A trade deficit is not proof that a country is open to trade. It is proof that it is spending more than its income or investing more than it saves.

For Stephen Roach, this is 'trade deficit disorder', which 'blames America's ills on trade deficits and the bad deals that underpin them'.[41]

Wolf and Roach's interpretations are simply a way of rearticulating the game theory aspects of trade: if country A imposes a tariff, country B will retaliate, so neither wins. And indeed, using trade openness indicators (total trade as a percentage of GDP), the United States appears less open than many of its counterparts (figure 3). While trade openness is a poor reflection of protectionism, it does give an indication of the role of trade in a country's economy: so Germany, because of the high trade component of its GDP, is more open (which could be interpreted as it being less protectionist).

The rhetoric is, again, too loose with the facts: it might better be called 'trade attention deficit disorder', since its effect is to distract attention away from the real challenge faced by the US economy, which is that it has too little saving and long-term infrastructure investment.

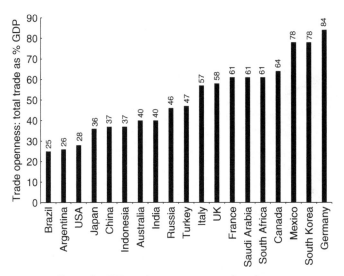

Figure 3. G20 trade openness: total trade as a
percentage of GDP. *Source*: World Bank (2017).

A strategic approach to trade would argue that, very
simply, what the US administration is doing is reconnecting trade policy with domestic policy as a means of
justifying action elsewhere. Steve Bannon defines this as
economic nationalism:

> A governing creed which has put the economic interests
> of multinational firms and a wealthy international elite
> above that of ordinary working class Americans.[42]

In other words, the trade behaviour of others is unfair
in that it disadvantages America. This, in itself, is

justification for a trade 'war'; and while the language heats up, our attention focuses on that, not on the fact that, actually, nothing has yet happened.

On the other side of the Atlantic, Theresa May's approach is designed similarly to divert attention away from the United Kingdom's diminishing global influence and issues closer to home such as flat wage growth. Her objective is to tie trade, security and national interests together in the same sentence. This was evident in Saudi Arabia when she brokered trade deals for UK arms manufacturers and spoke of UK security interests in the region. As she said to ITV on 4 April 2017:

> We have cooperated on trade, but also on security, helping to maintain security of the region, but also the security of the United Kingdom. It's in the British national interest.

The Article 50 letter hinted that UK cooperation with the EU on security matters (crime and terrorism in particular) would be weakened if no deal could be reached.

In contrast with Donald Trump, though, Theresa May cannot invoke the language of a trade war, or start one for that matter, not least because of her weakened position after the UK general election in June 2017. Even if the election result had been better for her, until she has negotiated the exit agreement from the EU it is unlikely that she would have been able to negotiate on trade. This means that she is using her 'doctrine' of a strong

– even 'moral' – nation state to rally her troops (both political and electoral) around the national interest while making it clear in foreign policy terms that the days of 'attempting to remake the world in our own image' are long gone.[43] Security participation then becomes part of the background noise that suggests a position of power. Once again, strategic interests and trade are linked through rhetoric.

The foreign policy shift: from economic nationalism to 'trade war'

It is the balance between domestic and overseas policy that is the key to how nationalism links to strategic trade. For Janan Ganesh this is potentially the essence of the disconnect between public perception of what popular nationalism is and what the government thinks is the correct response. In his words:

> History keeps forcing countries into this choice between significance abroad and retrenchment at home. ... Some of the voters now fingered as neo-imperialists would trade their nation's record of world grandeur for what might delicately be called a more familiar populism.[44]

In other words, the public wants their politicians to focus on domestic issues rather than global ones because that is where they see the real risks to their jobs, their lives and their livelihoods. As the head of a large City of London lobbying organization commented, 'trade policy is ultimately domestic'. In other words, the received – but possibly erroneous – wisdom is that trade policy is about protecting domestic industries and jobs, and not about strategic influence abroad.

However, this does not reflect the way in which trade is actually linked to power. It simply reflects the fact that politicians, through the era of 'borderless' or 'new' globalization, forgot to communicate the role that trade plays domestically. Particularly in the United States, they seem to have remembered its domestic role; in the words of a senior French advisor:

> Mixing trade with nationalism and war rhetorically is very dangerous. Their conflation has already led Britain out of the EU. Who knows what will happen in the States?

For a senior banker, the result of the current war-like language was almost inevitably a 'trade war': 'We are busy creating enemies of our trade partners. This makes it easier to pick a fight on a bilateral basis.'

Understanding transition: why has 'new' globalization made the link between trade and power explicit again?

From approximately the early 1990s, as the Cold War ended and technological development allowed companies to transfer ideas as well as goods across borders, politicians and the 'international elite' began to declare 'the end of history'.[45] This does not mean, of course, that there is, in the literal interpretation of Fukuyama's words, 'no more history'. Instead, he argues, the legitimacy of liberal democracy would prevail and the world would develop into a 'single, coherent and directional history' that ends, to paraphrase, without borders or totalitarian ideologies. Free trade and multilateral trade agreements were both a counterpart and a consequence of globalization.

In a similar fashion, globalization affected the character of war. As General Sir Rupert Smith has argued, war as a 'battle in a field between men and machinery, war as a massive deciding event in a dispute in international affairs: such a war no longer exists'.[46] Instead, 'new wars'[47] are distinguished from 'old wars' because they are not supported by the state but rather blur the lines between war, crime and human rights violation. They use new technologies and 'involve a myriad of international connections'. As such, they should be seen as a product of globalization.[48]

Arguably, the nationalism we see now and the link to war derive from this period. On the one hand, commentators extolled the benefits of free trade, borderless and ideology-free politics, and the internationalization of the individual. But meanwhile, Mary Kaldor uses the example of Kosovo and Bosnia Herzegovina to suggest that new conflicts were developing. According to her, these conflicts contained all the hallmarks inherent to globalization:[49] they were local and international, and they used modern technology. Through the media and social media, which the state no longer controls, their impact is magnified, as well as misinterpreted.

All this suggests that we are back to trade attention deficit disorder again. The 'victory' of liberalism over tyranny suggested nation states' usefulness was over,[50] so they took their eye off the domestic ball. There was no need to articulate the positive effects of globalization in public discourse because this was the domain of global businesses. In the words of one German politician, 'trade has been something that business does: politicians haven't cared and people keep out'. Soft cultural and diplomatic power was the essence of true global influence.[51] Why have 'Rule Britannia' when you could have 'Cool Britannia'?

This has economic consequences too. The 'new' phase of globalization, which was the product of new technology, reversed the 'Great Divergence' of the 'old' globalization of the period from 1870 onwards, creating a 'Great Convergence'.[52] Old globalization through the nation state explained why economic, political and military power was concentrated in the hands of so few. New globalization, where transport and information costs are so much lower, means that developing nations' share of trade – specifically that of

China, South Korea, India, Poland, Indonesia and Thailand – has increased rapidly, and in China's case it has overtaken that of the current incumbents (the United States, Japan and Germany) because of its proximity to many of those countries.

In Hirschman's terms, the 'dependent' nations have, indeed, found their own routes to gain power and influence, in economic terms at least. While the dominant powers before 1990 were celebrating the success of their models, others were learning to play the game more effectively using the technologies that had been transferred to them by those very incumbents who were now being out-competed.[53] It was either highly prophetic or just an observation at the time that can be applied now when Hirschman said:

> The British Empire is said to have been acquired in a fit of absent-mindedness. However that may be, it seems a more convincing proposition that empires, formal or informal, tend to crumble in that way.[54]

The problem with all of this hubris, even 'fetishization' of the process of change,[55] is that it neglects the people who have lost from the process. Even Fukuyama acknowledges that there will be winners and losers and, as the phenomena of Brexit, Trump and even the UK election in June 2017 tell us, those individuals who have lost out are angry and have found a voice. What the fantastic (in the literal sense of the word) view of globalization forgets is that, as the national identity of the individual is lost, the international structures and institutions that nominally replace the nation state lack any form of democratic legitimacy for ordinary voters: the 'somewheres'.[56] Finding a new identity from this global anomie[57] means that individuals have no social norms and no values that bind them. 'Global shift',[58] which maps out the intricate way in which economic relations are interdependent across the world, has become 'global drift', where individuals themselves feel detached, even alienated, from these intricate patterns.

Against this backdrop, the definition of a trade war may seem somewhat banal. Yet this is, arguably, the tool that politicians have picked up in invoking economic nationalism. If nation states no longer have unique control of the legitimate use of violence – and if, similarly, they have limited control over the operations of the businesses that undertake trade – then what better to do than to link foreign and domestic policy together in a trade war?

Trade, after all, is also a useful tool of foreign policy. Coercive diplomacy through sanctions can be used to force recalcitrant states into compliance with a global order that is dictated by the dominant economic power. Withdrawal of resources, revenues or investment is the ultimate soft-power 'stick'.[59] If power is the ability to get others to conform to your way of thinking, then a trade deal, a dose of foreign direct investment or a diplomatic and/or culture and trade mission may well do the trick. Failing that, the threat of sanctions may act as a strong incentive to fall into line.

For example, in the words of one interviewee:

> Sanctions are a signal of strategic intent and there are three types: sanctions against individuals or countries who divert from an 'accepted' path, 'classic' sanctions, where a country has broken trade rules, and a new type emerging: proxy sanctions where a country uses its own resources to wield power over another to express discontent with the actions of a third – like China's ban of travel to South Korea because it is unhappy with the THAAD deployment.[60]

Concluding remarks

This last interpretation takes us back full circle to the concept of the 'trade war': we can indeed use the phrase to mean a form of coercive action that convinces a nation, or indeed an individual, to act according to the will of another. To requote Clausewitz, that is, 'war is the continuation of policy by other means'.[61] The military uncertainty of the Cold War was replaced with the social and economic uncertainty of globalization's ruling liberal and international elite.

Another prophet, or close observer, was Dwight Eisenhower. In his 1961 farewell speech, he warned America of two things: first, that its, and the world's, military–industrial complex was more powerful at that point than at any point in history; and second, that technological change saw the rise of a 'technological elite' that could hijack social progress.[62]

Maybe populism as a backlash against an elite goes as far back as 1961, or maybe it is a function of globalization. Wherever the truth lies, the result now is the invocation of the power of the nation state and nationalism to replace the ideological void – and indeed identity void – that globalization left. This void creates the world of political, military and economic instability that has emerged since the financial crisis. Nothing is clear; and that uncertainty is equally present for the individual voter and for national politicians. Yet filling that void means a new 'contract' between the individual and the state. At present, that void is being filled by nationalism, which, logically, leads to trade wars.

In other words, the type of war this politics now creates is based on trade as a proxy for power. This means that we need to extend our definition of trade war. Let us be clear: we will not go to war over Germany's or China's trade surplus, and any economic tools that might be used as weapons to address those surpluses will be limited in their impact on trade itself, and indeed may prove negative for the aggressor anyway. However, the rhetorical weapons of a trade war have a greater fallout and threaten to damage the global free-trade system that has evolved. Now, in the febrile context of a prospective trade war, we could argue the same thing: that a return to economic nationalism and protectionism, if real, would create a similar mutually assured destruction in economic terms. That is, a trade war itself may well remain in the domain of rhetoric.

But strategic trade, as a means of – even a proxy for – war itself, will, as it has done throughout the internationalist continuum, remain a key part of the quest for influence. This is a different interpretation of trade's role that is explicitly linked to power in soft and hard terms and plays out in three ways.

- Key sectors will have both a civilian and a military function. These 'dual-use' goods constitute a large proportion of trade in developed and emerging economies and, as the following chapters show, are closely correlated with GDP. They are hence a measure of 'strategic intent'. These sectors include automotives, machinery, components and equipment, aerospace, pharmaceuticals and oil, which reflect both strategic influence and energy security.

- The defence sector, and specifically arms trade, is key to strategic intent and is again highly correlated with

GDP for the G20 countries. It therefore also serves both a military and a civilian purpose.

- The link between political instability and arms trade suggests a covert role for weapons trade in fighting proxy wars.

The policy consequences of this are clear. Generally speaking, trade as a 'benign' phenomenon is conducted by businesses, and the weaponization of language around trade is irresponsible. It creates an environment that potentially holds back corporate investment because of the threat of protectionism, instability or retaliation, and this threatens the successes that are evident in the post-war era.

Trade as a tool of foreign policy and grand strategy is similarly powerful. It is not clear, given the rhetoric surrounding trade at present, that all politicians are consciously aware of this. By weaponizing the language around trade, there is a risk that disagreements, even conflicts, intensify. This is in nobody's interest, still less a national one since it encourages isolationism and nationalism. National interest and national security are not bad things in themselves. Weaponized trade language is and should be avoided at all costs.

The focus for the rest of the book is on the role that strategic trade plays in creating political power and strategic influence. In the next three chapters we look at how trade has developed over the past twenty years and its role in generating soft and hard power. In chapters 5 and 6 we explore the importance of 'hidden' and dual-use goods trade in state strategy and the role of arms trade in political instability. Trade cannot and should not be seen just as an instrument of economic policy. The remainder of the book aims to demonstrate its link with power.

Chapter 4

Trade and power: the age-old relationship

The story so far

Trade is an essential component of political power and historically has defined the role of the nation state and its institutions – particularly its military–industrial complex. This means that trade and power are indistinguishable and, indeed, that strategic trade has the potential to transcend the soft–hard power dichotomy in that it provides states with a greater array of 'strategic choice'.[63] For example, a state could coerce using military means (hard power) or economic means (soft power), or it could export specific goods (e.g. arms) to a region in order to fuel an insurgency or undermine a regime. As a result, targeted exports of certain goods do not clearly belong to either 'hard' or 'soft' power. Instead, they find themselves in the realm of what we term strategic trade.

The previous chapter defined two ways in which strategic trade is important.

- Rhetorically: the rhetoric allows a policymaker to connect the domestic and foreign policy interests of the state. The use of trade in this manner constitutes coercive diplomacy; in invoking sanctions or the language of trade war, politicians appear to serve domestic interests while simultaneously influencing outcomes in foreign policy terms.
- Materially, in terms of strategic trade: this is particularly important in the emerging era of globalization, which has economic nationalism at its heart and is based on the failure of orthodox economic and military strategies. We argue that trade itself has the potential to represent the intentions of a state because of its sectoral focus, particularly in dual-use goods and arms.

Equally important was the period of globalization after the end of the Cold War, which was characterized by rapid technological change and a convergence of ideologies that, in international elite circles, gave rise to a perception of the 'end of the nation state' and the 'end of war'. For those outside the global elite this created a social void that was the precursor to the populism that has taken hold in many developed countries over the period since the financial crisis.

But populist politicians have noted a lack of identity as a source of frustration in their electorate. As a result, they have harnessed the rhetoric of economic nationalism in order to invoke a spirit of crisis and struggle – indeed, to identify an 'enemy' on the principle that, in the words of one senior banking interviewee, 'it's always easier to blame the neighbours'.

This struggle is arguably a 'moral panic'. That is, it is a 'condensed political struggle' to ensure that the less palatable products of globalization do not threaten existing power structures. Populists have seized on the 'blurred' distinction between immigrants, refugees and asylum seekers, terrorism and the rise of 'undesirable' nations to make their point.[64] This does not mean that these things are not an issue – far from it. But it does mean that the reaction 'is based on fantasy, hysteria, delusion and illusion'.[65] In other words, the *perception* that there is a threat from globalization and the products of globalization does not mean that there is an actual threat. It does mean, however, that the perception can be marshalled into a sense of outrage against globalization, and it is trade-based economic nationalism that has become the means through which that outrage is expressed.

The goal of this chapter is to demonstrate the relationship between trade and power. Power is a strong word with negative connotations as well as positive ones.

Trade plays a key role in creating hard and soft power and, more importantly, this is measurable through trade itself. However, the important point is that the more hard or soft power a country has through its economic and trade position, the more likely it is to use trade strategically. This is because the 'strategic choices' open to a country in terms of its international relations are broader.

Our focus is on the time period between 1996 and 2016, which broadly covers the two time frames associated most commonly with Baldwin's 'new' globalization and with our 'political' globalization defined in the previous chapters. It shows that on the face of it there was a decline in the value of arms trade globally, but that trade in the 'dual-use' sectors, which are more closely identified with strategic trade, increased. While this cannot be directly associated with an increase in military activity – since the goods are, by definition, for civilian purposes as well – it clearly measures the strategic intent of a nation state. In other words, the extent to which its soft power has hard power potential. The chapter concludes with a matrix of the link between hard and soft power through trade.

Trade power: what has changed?

So how much did trade change during the period of globalization? Was it really the case that trade grew but that the importance of the military–industrial complex declined? In other words, did trade in the goods directly associated with war actually decline?

Certainly, on the face of it, that appears to have been the case. Figure 4 shows arms trade as a percentage of total trade through the globalization era (1996–2016).

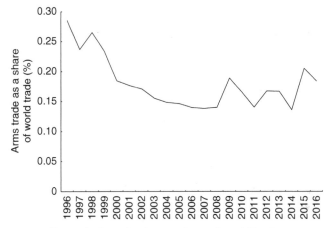

Figure 4. Arms trade as a share of world trade, 1996–2016 (%). *Source*: Equant Analytics, 2017.

The figure shows two things: first, that arms trade as a share of global trade has fallen back since 1996; and second, that since 2008 it appears to be growing again, albeit in a more volatile way. The percentage share of 0.21% of the value of world trade in 2015 was the highest for fifteen years, and while it would be a mistake to generalize from a 'trend' of one year, 2016's value is considerably higher than in 2008 and the same as in 2000.

Nevertheless, it seems that globalization did have some impact on the proportion of trade accounted for by arms. This does not mean that world arms trade has declined, however, and nor does it mean that arms trade is the only means through which goods that are used for military objectives are traded. Figure 5 shows the actual values of arms trade compared with dual-use goods trade between 1996 and 2016.

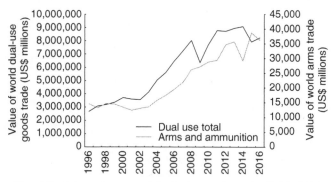

Figure 5. Value of arms and dual-use goods trade, 1996–2016 (millions of US dollars). *Source*: Equant Analytics, 2017.

Dual-use goods are defined by the EU as goods, software and technology that have both civilian and military applications and/or can contribute to the proliferation of weapons of mass destruction.[66] Care should be taken in interpreting their value because, by definition, these goods can be used for civilian purposes and are not necessarily traded with a military objective behind them. Because of this, it is likely that the value presented here will marginally overestimate the amount of dual-use goods trade that is used militarily.

This does not detract from the importance of the chart since our analysis shows that dual-use goods arguably proxy for the strategic intent of a nation, not least because technology is a critical component of military hardware and many of these sectors have strong technology elements. Both arms and dual-use goods trade grew in value terms during the period of globalization at a very similar rate. The only two exceptions were in 2009 and 2015. In these years there was also a significant drop in commodity prices, which explains the drop in dual-use goods trade (since many apparently ordinary commodities are used for military purposes as well), while arms trade continued to grow in value terms. The substantial drop in arms trade in 2014 was not related to oil or other commodity prices, nor was it necessarily related to a sudden decline in violence. There was, however, a tightening of sanctions against Russia in 2014, while the anti-money-laundering (AML) and Know Your Client (KYC) compliance backlash after the HSBC fines in 2012 also came into force in 2014. While the evidence is circumstantial, this seems more than coincidence.

Speculation aside, it is legitimate to conclude two things. First, arms trade is growing at a similar rate to dual-use goods trade globally. While arms trade has fallen back as a proportion of global trade, its growth has been substantial. Second, arms and ammunition are not the only routes through which materials used for military purposes are transmitted. While it is probable that dual-use goods data presented here overestimate the trade that is attributable purely to military objectives, the similar growth in arms trade over the period indicates that trade related to state strategy is both strong and growing. It may well be the case that world trade grew rapidly during the globalization era. However, it is not the case that military-related trade declined, suggesting that some sectors within the dual-use goods sector in particular are not economic, but rather have a political or strategic purpose.

This means that we should reexamine the assumption that the nature of the nation state changed during the globalization era. It stands to reason that if trade in what can only be described as strategic goods grew, there must have been countries for whom this trade was important. In other words, these countries still had power, not just in their overall trade (arguably reflecting their soft power) but also in their military trade, reflecting a harder, more strategic aspect to their trade.

To get to the real relationship between hard and soft power through trade, we need to take a proxy measure. Figures for dual-use goods, as already stated, overestimate the size of strategic trade in that they include goods that are also used for civilian purposes. However, they proxy well for the overall size of trade that is associated with state strategy, both in economic and military terms. In other words, it is the trade that is important for strategic influence and power. More specifically, it tells us a lot about how the character of strategy-related trade is changing since it includes, for example, telecommunications and security systems, nuclear materials and electronics.

Arms trade, in contrast, is directly linked to military activity, either directly in conflict or to deter against conflict. There are big differences in how imports and exports of each should be interpreted so we have taken total trade to give an overall indication of the importance of these sectors for each of the G20 economies.

For most of the G20, there are strong correlations between arms trade and GDP and between dual-use goods trade and GDP over the period of globalization between 1996 and 2016 (figure 6). The high correlation for most countries suggests that strategic trade has a strong association with economic growth. In itself this statement is unsurprising and, of course, says nothing about causality; it simply means that larger countries (here the G20 only) have larger sectors with strategic functions in both economic and political terms. In other words, the goods and services associated with a nation's defence are connected with its economic interests as well – for the G20 at least.

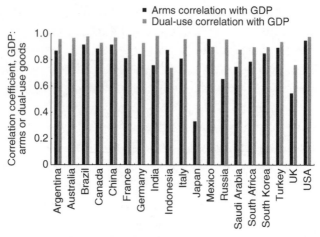

Figure 6. Correlation of GDP with arms trade and dual-use goods trade, 2000–2016 (coefficient value). *Source*: Equant Analytics/IMF, 2017. *Note*: this figure reports on the nineteen individual countries in the G20 but excludes the EU28. The same applies for figures 7–9.

There are some notable exceptions to this, however. The first is the United Kingdom. Here, the correlation of arms trade with GDP is just 0.55, while for dual-use goods the correlation is 0.77. Although the United Kingdom's trade is highly correlated with GDP overall (0.94), this suggests that sectors that are not associated with strategy or defence are more closely correlated. It might be inferred from this that the United Kingdom's military and economic interests are more separated than they are, say, in the United States or even in Germany or China. This may suggest a link to the importance of physical security as much as its link with GDP.

A second notable case is Japan, whose arms trade is similarly weakly correlated with its GDP. This is unsurprising given that Article 9 of their constitution, implemented in 1947, forbids the use of war as a means of mediating international disputes and Japan has therefore had a Self-Defence Force, not an army. Since the end of World War II, Japan has maintained a strategic culture of overt pacifism: they have been involved in only one conflict (in Iraq, where they deployed 1,000 troops in a non-combative role) and one UN-led anti-piracy mission (Operation Ocean Shield). Therefore, if we assume that arms proxy for use in, or protection against, direct conflict, the low correlation of arms trade with Japan's GDP begins to make sense. However, this does not suggest that strategic trade is unimportant for Japan: the correlation between dual-use goods trade and GDP is strong. That is, Japan has robust strategic intent even if it does not use the goods for military purposes overtly.

Two more interesting examples are Germany and China, who are regarded as 'soft' rather than 'hard' powers in that their global power emanates from their overall economic presence proxied through trade. However, both of these countries have correlations between arms trade and GDP and between dual-use goods trade and GDP that are extremely high. The reasons behind this differ: despite all its soft-power rhetoric, China's military expenditure amounted to $214 billion in 2015.[67] While this is half of the equivalent spent by the United

States, it dwarfs Germany's expenditure, or indeed the United Kingdom's.

Germany's case is interesting. Like Japan, its military has had a national defence remit since World War II. It also has constitutional restrictions through Article 26 on the use of force and against participation in 'wars of aggression'. In fact, until recently it has been unable to discuss the link between strategic interests, business and trade: when Horst Köhler, the then German president, stated in 2010 that Germany's involvement in Afghanistan was protecting its trade interests, the public outcry was so great that he had to resign. This may explain why the relationship between its arms trade and GDP is weaker than it is for China. However, the relationship is still very strong and this is because Germany is a major manufacturer and exporter of arms equipment as well as of dual-use goods. Crucially, this is not overtly attributed to Germany's foreign policy, which is constrained by its post-war constitution. As a result, this power has to be seen as economic. This explains the close correlation with GDP, but, unlike China, its power remains soft (at least for now).

Similarly, India is highly militarized and its trade is strategic around core sectors such as iron and steel and technology. It has several ongoing insurgencies, such as those in Jammu and Kashmir, it has a strong strategic nuclear programme and a strong military and airforce, and it is engaged in a 'war of nerves' with Pakistan.

This is reflected in the relatively high arms trade–GDP correlation.

Dual-use goods and arms trade shed some further light on why the rates of growth in India and Argentina are so high. Figure 7 ranks growth in a country's arms trade by its compound annualized growth rate (CAGR) for the period 1996–2006, since this shows the key changes between that first 'pure globalization' period and the second 'financial crisis globalization' period of 2007–16. As noted above, trade in arms at a global level did not fall back in 2009, unlike trade in other sectors, so this latter grouping is not distorted by the crisis.

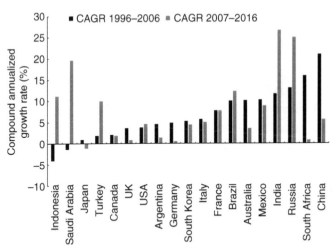

Figure 7. G20 arms trade growth (CAGR), 1996–2006 and 2007–2016 compared (%). *Source*: Equant Analytics, 2017.

By ranking the G20 growth based on the earlier time period, figure 7 shows where arms trade is growing most from a modest or negative base. For example, Indonesia's arms trade growth was negative between 1996 and 2006 but grew extremely rapidly between 2007 and 2016. Saudi Arabia's arms trade growth in the second period compared with the first is even more dramatic. Turkey's arms trade also shows the same, more rapid, growth in the second period, while Russia and India, albeit from a stronger growth base in the first period, have also shown greater growth in the second.

It would be misleading to classify India's or Indonesia's arms trade growth as the same as that for Saudi Arabia, Turkey or Russia. Arms trade is growing from a very low base in the case of the former two countries, which is not true for Saudi Arabia or Russia, and increasingly not for Turkey either. The involvement of Saudi Arabia, Turkey and Russia in conflicts in the Middle East is reflected in their arms trade and, hence, can be interpreted as a reflection of their respective strategies for the region.

China presents an interesting case. Its arms trade growth was particularly marked in the first period, as it built the military strength that we see now. This arguably reflects the multipolarization and convergence of growth in the globalization period that was discussed in chapter 2. However, what is equally marked is the slowdown in growth (albeit from a larger base) in the second period from 2007. This reflects the capacity of China to produce arms itself, since import growth slowed from an annualized rate of 22% in the first period to just over 7% in the second. It also reflects the shift in China's state strategy towards demand-led growth and a pattern of consumption more consistent with a mid-income economy. Furthermore, it is signalling a more assertive foreign policy through its actions in the South China Sea and through the 'one belt, one road' policy. These are both important in broadening the country's trade reach, securing energy supplies and increasing maritime influence.[68]

All of this suggests that there is, for many countries, intrinsic 'hard power' within their trade relationships with other countries. We can see that all the G20 powers, with the notable exception of Germany, have substantial arms trades that proxy for strategic intent – and, furthermore, that arms trade has grown rapidly throughout the period of globalization.

This does not paint the whole picture, however. The problem is that we cannot generalize from the G20. China's military power is well proxied through its growth in arms trade because the increase has been substantial; indeed, China's recent military expenditure rivals that of the developed nation states like the United States, Germany, the United Kingdom and France. The growth in Germany's arms trade is worth a special mention in the context of its constitutional framework. Germany is constitutionally limited to defence of its borders and this has defined the way in which its foreign policy has been formulated in the post-World War II period. It is a large exporter of arms, showing that the influence it wields through strategic trade allows it to promote its strategic interests abroad without explicitly spending money on its own army or engaging them directly.

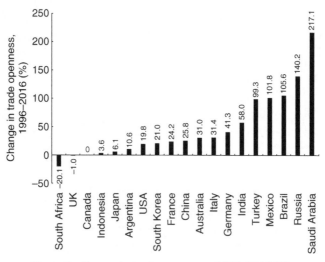

Figure 8. Change in trade openness, 1996–2016 (%).
Source: Equant Analytics, IMF 2017.[69]

It is worth exploring the role that strategic trade plays in generating soft power in more detail. Much was made in chapter 3 about the fact that trade openness – in other words, total trade as a percentage of GDP – is used as a measure of the extent to which a country is protectionist. It follows, therefore, that a less protectionist country has greater soft power, since its economic strength is more closely tied to its trade performance (figure 8).

The fastest-growing nations in terms of trade openness are, perhaps unsurprisingly, Brazil, Russia, India, Turkey, Mexico and Saudi Arabia. Such growth has given these newly emerging trading nations their place in the G20, which is arguably a political grouping as well as an economic one. But what is interesting about this chart is how the United Kingdom's trade openness has shrunk over the period while the growth in trade openness in the United States is lower than that in either China or Germany.

As always, this sort of finding should be treated with care. The United Kingdom's trade has been sluggish since the financial crisis and has struggled to get back to its nominal levels in 2008, while GDP has grown because of strong domestic demand. The United Kingdom remains a more open economy than the United States or China, with a trade to GDP ratio of 42.3% (figure 3).

As hinted at above, it is Germany that really exhibits the strongest soft power through trade, and this is important in a country whose foreign policy and military expenditure are constitutionally restricted. It is the most open economy of the G20 and the world's third largest trading nation in terms of exports and imports after the United States and China. However, the United States and China have unrestricted militaries that back up their otherwise 'soft' power. Germany, despite being a significant strategic partner, invests just 1.2% of its GDP in its military, well under the 2% NATO threshold. Yet the importance of its strategic trade means that its foreign policy and its trade policy are both clearly aligned with national interest. Furthermore, in the words of one senior politician:

> We see, and increasingly the German public sees, that we need to take our soft power seriously, indeed take up the responsibility that we have both in NATO and in Europe for security, particularly once the UK is no longer part of the EU. But we can't invest in our military – not just because of German public opinion. Our GDP is huge – can you imagine the size of our army if we spent 2% of it on military? You might find that others have a problem with that as well.

Germany's role as the answer to the Kissinger question – 'Who do I call if I want to talk to Europe?' – has become accepted in the period since the financial crisis and the Eurozone crisis: European power has shifted from a Franco-German axis to Berlin. While some may attribute this to a conflict of underlying ideologies and economic philosophies,[70] the truth is that the German economy has withstood the various crises since 2008 better than the French, and that is largely down to trade. This gives it a global soft power that, however reluctantly, it has had to accept as its duty, arguably to protect its national interests since Germany's future is bound with Europe for historical reasons.[71]

Conceptualizing hard and soft power through trade

What all of this means is that we can construct a matrix of the G20 that shows the relationship between hard and soft power (see figure 9). This is a stylized representation but nevertheless provides a picture of how trade and hard and soft power are linked to the nation state. We put soft power on the vertical axis (from weak to strong) and hard power on the horizontal axis. Soft power is seen as a function of trade value and trade openness, while hard power is proxied through the correlation between arms trade and GDP and dual-use goods as a share of total trade.

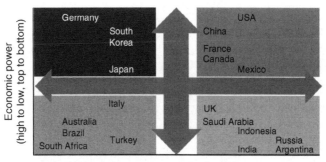

Figure 9. The trade-based soft power–hard power matrix.

To be clear, we are using trade in dual-use goods as a proxy for strategic intent in this context. We could perhaps have used military expenditure, but the point we are making is that, as was shown in the case of Germany, military expenditure is only a partial picture of that strategic intent and, hence, dual-use goods trade is a better proxy.

This approach puts Germany, South Korea and Japan largely into the top left-hand corner of the quadrant showing strong trade but weaker actual hard power. The United States, in contrast, is at the top of the hard and soft power quadrant: it is the world's second largest trading nation (and the largest importer) but it is not as open as, say, Germany; the correlation between GDP and arms is very high.

China is the interesting one to place: it is the world's largest trading nation and yet it is quite closed. Its implicit hard power, represented through dual-use and arms trade, places it in the hard power quadrant, despite the fact that rhetorically and diplomatically it presents itself as a soft power. And the United Kingdom is the most challenging of all to place: it is the world's sixth largest importer and tenth largest exporter, meaning that its soft power is relatively weak, howsoever open it may be. Alongside this, the correlation between arms trade and GDP is weaker than for many other countries, although the proportion of trade accounted for by dual-use goods is the highest among the G20, suggesting that trade in dual-use goods and arms is a key component of its strategy. In other words, 'strategic trade', e.g. with Saudi Arabia, helps it achieve influence without direct military engagement. This places it towards the centre of the matrix with a bias towards hard power.

Summary

There is, then, no real evidence that the trade power of the world's most established nation states has diminished over the period. We have used arms trade as a proxy for direct engagement and evidence of confrontational 'hard' foreign policy observed in a country's trade statistics. Dual-use goods trade proxies for the 'strategic intent' of a nation. Neither has diminished as a proportion of any country's total trade over the period of globalization, and this suggests that there is no evidence that either confrontational foreign policy or the strategic intent of the nation state has diminished through the period of globalization. Indeed, growth in dual-use goods and arms trade was at its fastest during the period when globalization hubris was at its greatest: before the financial crisis. It seems that countries like Turkey, Saudi Arabia, Russia and even Mexico and Brazil have seen substantial arms trade growth. Particularly for Turkey, Saudi Arabia and Russia, this reflects the tensions within the Middle East and in the Central European/Central Asian arena.

This leads us to conclude that globalization provided the nation state with new tools to achieve strategic influence, other than conventional military means. In other words, the lines between what is civilian and what is military became blurred during globalization; this is the essence of the growth in dual-use goods trade through the period. However, the rise of a country like China through the period of globalization does provide evidence to support the idea that the 'Western' (for want of a better term) nations have suffered from the trade attention deficit disorder we talked about in chapter 3. They were so focused on the size of the Chinese market and the opportunities that arose from globalization that they perhaps did not link that rising soft power with an equivalent rise in hard power.

There are danger signs in the data as well. Russia, Turkey and Saudi Arabia have always had 'hard power', but they now show signs of greater aspirations to 'hard power' in their arms trade but not their dual-use goods trade. This suggests that these countries are driven by 'conflict and confrontational' foreign policies and that these are at the base of the uncertainties and geopolitical conflicts we see now. That is, their strategic intent is driven to a greater extent by the fact that their trade is less diversified and, hence, is driven by geopolitics and is intrinsically less predictable.

We use the word 'geopolitics' with some caution because it is another term that is used in a loose manner by commentators. It is not the same as politics, which has been the subject of the narrative so far, in that we have looked at the links between foreign policy, strategy and trade. Rather, geopolitics refers to power relations that are inherently geographical in nature. It concerns borders, boundaries and resources: that is, the politics of territory and resource control. This is inherently strategic and, indeed, geography is a permanent feature of strategy. Similarly, trade is also about resources, and is therefore intrinsically geopolitical and strategic. This means there is a permanent and observable measure of state strategy in the trade data. The reason for defining geopolitics here is because it is very often confused with politics to refer to events like the US election or Brexit, or even terrorism. Fundamentally, geopolitics underpins the identity void and the fear that have caused individuals to feel insecure about their future.

Trade generally, and strategic trade in particular, is intrinsically geopolitical in that it is about allocation and control of resources across borders. It is the mechanism through which power and influence are exerted but this link with both political influence and geopolitical power is only now becoming explicit through the weaponized language that is being used. With that power, however, comes responsibility: to provide stability for global businesses on the one hand, and not to provoke others into retaliatory action on the other. It is not clear that this is obvious to key policymakers around the world.

Chapter 5

Trade, power and risk perception

It seems that the strategic intent of the nation state did not diminish during the period of globalization and while trade wars in the economic sense of the phrase were less important, trade as a vehicle for war was as important as ever. This is the new 'strategic trade war' that we began to define at the end of the last chapter.

- 'Old wars' are industrial wars, fought between nation states with sizable military–industrial complexes in support.

- 'New wars': this term is used with some caution since it is controversial in the literature, but it is characterized by asymmetry, insurgencies and counter-insurgencies that are not necessarily between nation states.

- 'Strategic trade wars' have emerged as a result of Western failures in recent conflicts. They use trade as a vehicle for coercion – either through orthodox trade wars (protectionism and sanctions) or through targeted trade in specific sectors with specific countries. This does not necessarily involve direct conflict (although it also does not preclude it) but it still bears the hallmarks of war in that it is politics by other means.

What is particularly interesting about 'strategic trade' and wars fought through it is that they are not necessarily new, and indeed, as the last chapter showed, they increased in frequency during the period between 1996 and 2014.

Yet somehow, through the twenty years between 1996 and 2016 politicians have felt the need to reassert their dominance over the concept of the nation state. This is their response to the observable frustration and anger with the globalization process among the voting public. Economic nationalism, through trade, revolves around the soft power associated with global influence. This is ultimately a response to perceived uncertainties and risks that have appeared to become more acute since the financial crisis.

This post financial crisis era cannot be called post-globalization, however much our politicians may want to present themselves as 'anti-globalization'. Trade growth has flattened since 2010, but the use of technology – specifically digital technology – is changing the way we work, the way we do business and, indeed, the way we define ourselves as businesses and individuals. Any company with a website is arguably internationally visible, even if it does not formally 'export'. In reality, digitization and telecommunications mean that globalization has become so embedded that the clocks simply cannot be turned back.

This is a reaction to the current uncertainties in the world that have themselves emerged as a result of the globalization process. Ernest Gellner argued that the nation state, as a collection of institutions with shared cultural and social values (i.e. nationalism), would logically emerge from the pre-industrial morass of loosely connected groups and interests whose actions were uncoordinated and random. The process of industrialization itself created the modern nation state, which marshalled resources, control and citizens around one identity.[72]

There is a resounding familiarity to this theme. Has globalization not itself created loose collections of interest groups around religion, ideologies and territories that fight for recognition or domination of resources? Might this not be the reason why individuals themselves feel unaligned and displaced? And if this is the case, is a reinvocation of nationalism, through the weaponization of trade, not the logical – if 'irrational'[73] – response?

This chapter looks at the structure of strategic trade to argue that trade itself has become the weapon with which these new wars have been fought and enabled. This strategic trade lens also allows us to understand why there is so much uncertainty – so many 'known unknowns'. For example, there is around $2.1 trillion of hidden trade in the global system at any one point in time.[74] Where better to hide a stolen car than in a car park? And where better to hide trade fraud, trade crime and trade weaponization than in the trade data itself?

This is not an attempt to build a conspiracy theory of world trade, and nor are we apportioning any responsibility. We simply report on facts. Nation states control the institutions (even weapons) of trade (customs and excise, tariff and regulatory regimes, and taxation, for example). It is not our intention to suggest that there is any direct involvement of a nation's military–industrial complex in any deliberate activity, but it is important to distinguish between what is observable strategic intent in the previous chapter and what might be called covert action in this.

Before we get carried away with the James Bond 'Universal Exports' or John le Carré *Night Manager* analogies, let us take a look at how big the problem is.

Hidden trade

The analysis is based on the Equant Analytics trade database, which covers goods and services trade for 200 countries and for every sector flow between those countries for 12,800 products and sectors. But in contrast to, say, the United Nations, from which its data is derived, or the WTO or the OECD, it mirrors each bilateral trade flow. This means that otherwise-hidden trade becomes visible. For example, Saudi Arabia is notoriously bad at reporting its data, but Germany is not. By looking at Germany's trade with Saudi Arabia, we get a much clearer idea of what Saudi Arabia itself is doing.

This has the effect of reconstructing the data for the countries that report poorly, many of which are in the regions where wars and conflicts are prevalent. The Equant Analytics divergence ratio (EADR) is the difference between what a country reports that it is trading with the UN and what Equant Analytics finds it is actually trading, found by mirroring the data (figure 10).

The average divergence over time for the world is 12%. This varies from year to year (in 2015, for example, it was 17%), but since 1996 it is fair to say that without the mirroring process, the world has mislaid an average of 12% of its trade values each year. The divergence ratio is weighted to reflect the relationship between exports and imports for any one country. It is usually in a country's interest to record its import data more accurately, because it receives tax revenues from imports, so by weighting for exports and imports as a proportion of total trade, we get an accurate picture of the real divergence ratio. This gives a slightly lower figure than for just exports.

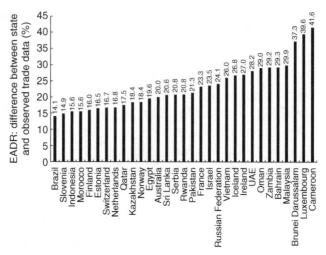

Figure 10. Above-average divergence between stated, or recorded, data with UN Comtrade and observed data from mirroring, 2015 (%). *Source*: Equant Analytics, 2017.

The data in figure 10 are for those countries that have higher than average divergences and actual data recorded with the UN for 2015 (there were too few at the time of writing to conduct the analysis for 2016). There are an equal number of countries that have no data for 2015 registered with the UN – all of their data are reconstructed through the mirroring process and we will come back to that shortly.

The biggest nation states, arguably with the most to lose in soft power terms, are actually very good at recording their data and are therefore not visible in the chart. For example, Germany's EADR is just 2.8%, while the United Kingdom and the United States are similar at 4.6%. Even China, whose reputation for data reliability has been questioned, has an EADR of 10.5%, which is still below average.

Macao, in contrast, has an EADR of 49.7%. The UAE has a divergence ratio of 28.2%, with Saudi Arabia at 50.5%, and Cyprus and Malta, which act as trading posts for companies wanting to trade with Russia and the Middle East, at divergence ratios of 81% and 201.4%, respectively. Interestingly, Luxembourg also has a high divergence ratio, at 30.6%. It is a major financial centre, so while trade may be booked through that country, it does not necessarily get processed through customs and excise and therefore recorded with the UN. The same is true for Switzerland, whose weighted EADR was 16.7% in 2015 but whose EADR for imports in 2014 was 63%.

Some countries, particularly in Africa and the Middle East, have exceptionally high EADRs for 2015. These are consistent and relatively stable over time, suggesting that their data recording is just weak. However, other countries, like Switzerland, have EADRs that are volatile (as shown in the example above). This volatility reflects trade between years. For example, we found that Switzerland's high import EADR in 2014 was a result of its oil and gas imports from Russia, valued at over $150 billion. This distortion fell out in the 2015 figure.

We can use a case of hidden trade to illustrate the interface between foreign and trade policy. It stands to reason to assume that no country explicitly trades with North Korea except China, and, even then, Chinese trade has to comply with global sanctions. Indeed, since the North Korean nuclear tests, the United States has been very tight on ensuring that China imposes those sanctions more rigorously, particularly when it comes to any products that might be used in North Korea's nuclear programme.[75] Yet that nuclear programme appears well supported by its imports in two dual-use goods sectors: nuclear and aerospace and propulsion (figure 11).

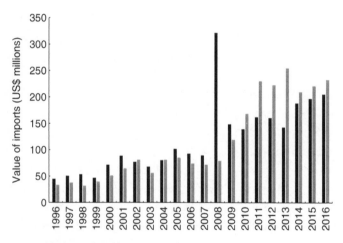

- Nuclear-related imports   Aerospace and propulsion imports

Figure 11. Value of North Korea's imports of nuclear-related and aerospace and propulsion dual-use goods, 1996–2016 (millions of US dollars). *Source*: Equant Analytics, 2017.

The chart shows a marked increase in imports of nuclear-related dual-use goods in 2008 ahead of North Korea's second test in 2009, and a significant and sustained increase in aerospace and propulsion dual-use goods between 2011 and 2013, marking Kim Jong-un's ascendancy and assumption of power in 2012. This bilateral trade relationship represents a bargaining tool for both North Korea and, arguably, China, since 95% of the trade in these goods is from China. In other words, this trade is strategic. While it is unlikely to lead to large-scale war, it is 'one step removed' in that it potentially reflects the strategic interests of both countries.

We argued at the outset that who trades what and with whom is important, and strategic trade is (sometimes necessarily) covert, in the national interest. In other words, it goes to destinations that are not 'formal' countries as such but that can hold strategic goods. Four of these destinations, with their UN definitions, are listed below.[76]

- The first category is called 'Areas Not Elsewhere Specified' ('Areas NES').[77] It is used (a) for low-value trade, (b) if the partner designation was unknown to the exporting country, or (c) if an error was made in the partner assignment. The reporting country does not provide the details of its intended trading partner in these specific cases. Sometimes reporters do this to protect company information. This category constituted around $65 billion in 2016 but it is not possible to define which countries these are as they are too small or are unknown.

- 'Bunkers' are 'ship stores and aircraft supplies, which consist mostly of fuels and food'. Trade in this category amounted to around $3.2 billion in 2016. These bunkers are floating vessels and off-shore constructions rather than land mass in their own right.

- 'Special categories' are 'used by a reporting country if it does not want the partner breakdown to be disclosed'. Special categories accounted for around $4.2 billion of trade in 2016.

- 'Free zones' that 'belong to the geographical and economic territory of a country but not to its customs territory. For the purpose of trade statistics, the transactions between the customs territory and the free zones are recorded. Free zones can be commercial free zones (duty free shops) or industrial free zones.' The data suggest that this trade constituted around $2.3 billion in 2016.

All together, these categories comprised just over 4% of world trade in 2016, amounting to more than $75 billion.

The UN definitions themselves refer to the strategic nature of these categories: countries may want to protect the supplier or the buyer, and these categories are designed specifically for that. So, what does their trade look like? What is being traded and with whom? The categories of Areas NES and Bunkers have the most consistent data so we focus on them, looking first at Areas NES.

Two things are striking about figure 12: first, and most obviously, across the time period, Areas NES have imported considerably more than they have exported; and second, imports and exports seem to be inversely related since the financial crisis in 2007/8, suggesting that this category is being used as a place for storing commodities rather than for exporting. This theory is borne out by the largest sectors traded (figure 13): commodities not elsewhere specified, oil and gas, and aircraft.

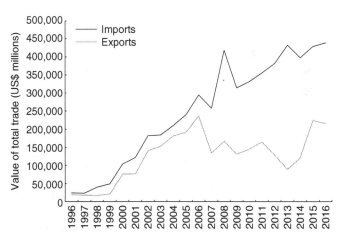

Figure 12. Value of imports and exports for Areas NES, 1996–2016 (millions of US dollars). *Source*: Equant Analytics, 2017.

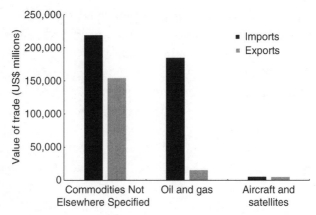

Figure 13. Value of top three sector trade for Areas NES, 2016 (millions of US dollars). *Source*: Equant Analytics, 2017.

The trade 'deficit' of Areas NES is quite clear here, as is the concentration in oil and gas and commodities not elsewhere specified (commodities NES). Here are a few interesting facts about this hidden trading partner, Areas NES.

- The correlation coefficient between Areas NES monthly trade and the oil price is 0.78.
- Areas NES is Russia's largest export partner.
- Exports of works of art from Areas NES are worth $6.3 billion, while ore, slag and waste imports are worth over $22 billion. These are sectors commonly associated with fraud.

Similarly, commodities NES is also a new sector that we have not hitherto encountered and it is worth dwelling on it for a moment. There is no formal definition on the UN website to describe what is in commodities NES, except to say that they are commodities that are not defined according to kind. The category's vital statistics follow below.

- In 2016 its total value was around $1.13 trillion, or nearly 6% of world trade, which is even higher than the trade that goes to more obscure 'partners'.
- The correlation coefficient between dual-use goods trade and commodities NES is 0.91.
- The correlation coefficient between arms trade and commodities NES is 0.77.
- The UAE imports the most and Areas NES imports the second most 'commodities NES' in the world.
- Areas NES exports the most and the UAE the second most commodities NES in the world.

All of this suggests that there is some link between informal, or covert, strategy and trade within some of the less transparent trade flows in the world. There are two areas of national interest that are potentially significant in this respect: first, strategic influence and power, which helps explain the high correlation with arms trade; and second, energy security, which helps explain the correlation with oil prices.

Further evidence of the role of energy security in these unconventional sectors is shown by looking more closely at the category Bunkers. Bunkers imports but barely exports and its largest traded sector is oil and gas. In fact, oil and gas is so large in this sector that other areas are dwarfed in comparison. Even so, within its top ten are commodities NES and arms and ammunition. The monthly movements of Bunkers trade with oil prices yield a correlation coefficient of 0.63 (figure 14) and this, along with the trade with Areas NES, suggests that taking oil into and out of circulation in this way may have a direct impact on the oil price.

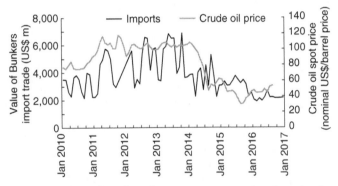

Figure 14. Value of Bunkers imports versus crude oil spot price, January 2010–January 2017 (millions of nominal US dollars or US dollars per barrel). *Source*: Equant Analytics, 2017/Statistica, 2017.

Two things are immediately obvious from this chart. The first is that while oil prices were higher up to mid 2014, imports into Bunkers were erratic but broadly moved up and down with oil prices. Since the oil price drop, however, a second thing is noticeable: trade is more stable and has fallen back in dollar terms.

This may seem like a digression away from trade wars and the weaponization of trade. But it certainly is not. Energy security, or more specifically the control of oil supply, is at the heart of geopolitics, and the uncertainties about what is being traded and with whom are quite clear from the material presented so far. What is even more evident is that even if there is no covert activity directing trade to more obscure destinations, the customs authorities – because the trade is reported to the UN – will know what is happening. We have obtained this information by mirroring the data between the most reliable reporters and their less reliable counterparts. In other words, this is the trade that is well reported and may actually fall within the 'legal' frameworks of the institutions of the nation state and its trade. All of this points to the complexity of trade and its relationship with the geopolitical uncertainties that are endemic to world politics.

A note on the effect of sanctions

It has already been noted that much of the divergence in the trade that Switzerland reported to the UN in 2014 and what we observed in the data was because of oil and gas trade that was booked through Switzerland by Russia. This was the year in which US and European sanctions were imposed as a result of Russia's actions in Ukraine. Linking the highly divergent data with the imposition of sanctions indicates that sanctions were having a diversion effect. Imports into Areas NES fell too, and we similarly saw a drop in arms trade in 2014, consistent with sanctions against Russia.

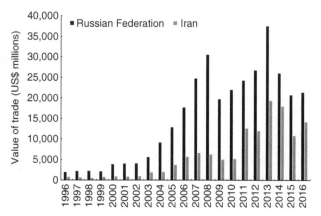

Figure 15. Turkey's imports from Russia and Iran. *Source*: Equant Analytics, 2017.

Sanctions are a popular tool of coercive diplomacy and Iran and North Korea, in different ways, show how they impact the overall trading position of a nation. Iran, for example, has had strong trade despite sanctions, because of its relationships with Turkey and Russia. Turkey acts as a conduit for sanctioned trade between Europe, Russia and the Middle East, and this is reflected in the fact that its top import partners are Iraq, Iran, Saudi Arabia, Israel and Russia (figure 15). The volatile trade with Iran since 2012 reflects the EU's embargo on Iranian oil, and the subsequent drop in trade with all partners, particularly marked since 2014, reflects both the tightening of AML and KYC and the drop in oil prices.

This is also reflected in Iran's trade with the world, which, although substantial, has fallen back considerably since 2012 (figure 16).

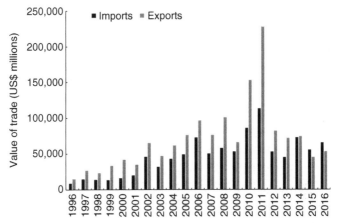

Figure 16. Value of Iran's trade, 1996–2016 (millions of US dollars). *Source*: Equant Analytics, 2017.

The impact of the EU's oil embargo on Iran's trade is particularly marked here. The pick-up in 2016 may simply be because of the slight improvement in commodity prices. It is unlikely that anticipation of the end of sanctions towards the close of President Obama's presidency would have had much impact on the overall trade figures. This is not least because US regulators still restrict trade finance relations with any Iranian bank that may have links to the nuclear programme. While this remains the case, it will be extremely difficult for banks elsewhere to facilitate trade directly if they wish to remain compliant with US regulations. Given the current US administration's position towards Iran, it is very unlikely that there will be any change in this position. This gives some indication of why nation states may want to have some ... shall we say 'less transparent' trade partners.

Case study 1: Russia and the United Kingdom's trade with Syria

A more detailed case study of Syria and its relationship with Russia and the United Kingdom reinforces this view of strategic trade. We see evidence, particularly in Russia's exports to Syria, of trade fuelling the Syrian conflict.

In 2011 widespread pro-democracy protests took place across the Middle East in what became known as the Arab Spring. In Syria these protests escalated after Bashar al-Assad's forces opened fire on protesters. The protesters began arming themselves in response and soon split into several rebel groups in violent opposition to Assad's regime. As the war progressed the conflict developed a sectarian element, with Sunnis clashing with Alawites and Islamic State growing in influence. Since 2011, roughly 250,000 Syrians have lost their lives, millions have been displaced, and the country's economy has all but collapsed as fighting has intensified (figure 17). Sanctions against Assad also took their toll as members of the international community ceased trading with a regime they could not support. For example, we can see in figure 18 how the United Kingdom's total trade with Syria severely declined between 2009 and 2016. In value terms, the drop was from nearly $300 billion in 2009 to just $13 million in 2016 – or, as a percentage, a 95.5% reduction in trade.

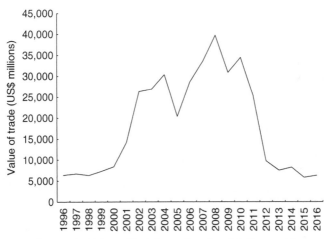

Figure 17. Value of Syria's total trade with the world (millions of US dollars). *Source*: Equant Analytics, 2017.

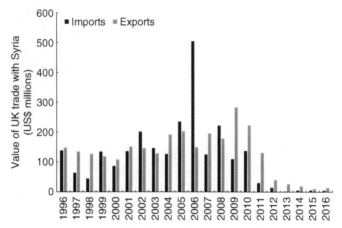

Figure 18. UK trade with Syria, 1996–2016 (millions of US dollars). *Source*: Equant Analytics, 2017.

However, trade with Syria has not disappeared completely (see figure 17). In 2014 Jihad Yazigi wrote that the country had transitioned to a 'war economy' and that goods entering the country were prolonging the conflict, with regime-controlled areas still enjoying 'the provision of many basic state services'.[78] Russia openly backs Assad and his campaign to regain control, and since 2010 it has provided the majority of the incoming goods. As figure 19 shows, Russia's trade with Syria increased by 46% between 2014 and 2015. By comparison, the United Kingdom's exports to Syria fell by 40% over the same period. Furthermore, instead of a drop in trade as civil war broke out, we see a 72.1% increase in Russia's exports to Syria between 2010 and 2011.

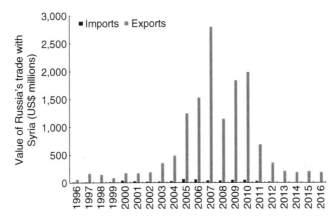

Figure 19. Value of Russia's trade with Syria, 1996–2016 (millions of US dollars). *Source*: Equant Analytics, 2017.

Russia's strategy in the Middle East revolves around keeping Assad in power; it would be incorrect to assume that this is because they are politically aligned, however. Rather, Russia has interests in protecting its naval base in Tartus; in January 2017 Russia signed a 49-year deal granting them full control of the base, which is capable of hosting up to eleven warships and is in a key strategic location in the Mediterranean. Furthermore, by intervening in the region while the United States and NATO would not, Russia is sending a strong signal to current Middle Eastern regimes that *they*, not NATO, are the most reliable security actors in the region.

Russia's current strategy towards Syria is reflected in the goods it is exporting there. Figure 20 looks at Russia's top ten exports to Syria in 2016 and compares their value with their values in 2002 as evidence of Russia's changing strategy towards the country over the period.

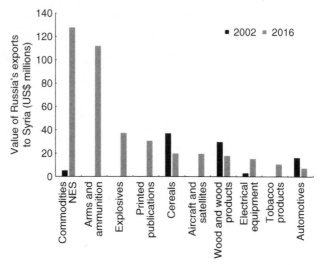

Figure 20. Value of Russia's top ten exports to Syria: a comparison of 2002 with 2016 (millions of US dollars). *Source*: Equant Analytics, 2017.

In 2016, $128 million of Russia's exports to Syria were in commodities NES while a further $111 million were in arms and ammunition and $37 million were in explosives; compare this with a total value of just $5 million for these sectors in 2002. Furthermore, within the sectors 'printed publications' and 'electrical equipment' are dual-use goods including instruction manuals and blueprints as well as electronic triggers for weapons systems. Meanwhile, Russia's trade in more benign sectors such as cereals, wood and wood products, and automotives fell from a total value of $83 million in 2002 to $45.2 million in 2016: further evidence of Syria's war economy.

So, if Russia is protecting its interests by trading directly with the Syrian government, the next question to ask is: how can the United Kingdom influence proceedings within Syria without direct military engagement or trading directly with the country? The answer is to trade by proxy. In other words, to use neighbouring states as conduits to achieve their strategic objectives. The United Kingdom has had cordial relations with Saudi Arabia since 1915, when the Treaty of Darin was signed, and the country is viewed by the United Kingdom as one of the more stable and trustworthy countries in the region. Given this relationship and the country's advantageous strategic location, the relationship with Saudi Arabia is seen as integral to British security interests in the Middle East (figure 21).

There are three striking aspects of figure 21.

- Arms and ammunition trade was not in the top ten traded sectors in 2002, but by 2016 it was the fourth largest sector. This sector includes small arms and ammunition rather than components for sophisticated weapons systems, which are found in other sectors, including aircraft and satellites and electrical equipment (the second and fifth largest export sectors in 2016).

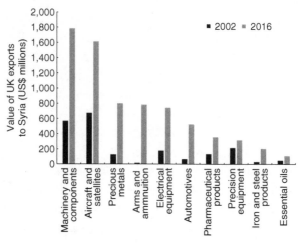

Figure 21. Value of the United Kingdom's top ten exports to Saudi Arabia: 2002 and 2016 compared (billions of US dollars). *Source*: Equant Analytics, 2017.

- The sectors all have high dual-use content: machinery and components, for example, includes computing, data storage and digital detection systems, while electrical equipment includes semi-conductors and electronic monitoring systems. In other words, many of the products included in these sectors are associated with defence and security systems.

- The substantial increase in precious metal trade between 2002 and 2016 is largely the result of increased direct gold exports from the United Kingdom to Saudi Arabia. While this sector includes precious metals used in high-end electronic equipment manufacture, it is predominantly bullion.

It appears that the respective policy positions of Russia and the United Kingdom in relation to the conflict in Syria are reflected in the trade data. We can see evidence of a change in strategy from both states over our time period, highlighted not only by trends in total exports but also by *what* is being traded, and with whom.

Summary

This chapter has focused on strategic trade's covert intent: to promote a country's strategic interests on the one hand and to ensure energy security on the other. The high correlation with 'hidden' trade and the oil price illustrates how energy security and oil prices are linked through trade with some of the world's more obscure trading partners (particularly Areas NES and Bunkers).

However, the chapter has also hinted at the importance of the strategic influence that is developed through specific types of trade. The example of North Korea's trade illustrates how North Korea and China both benefit from their strategic trade relationship in dual-use goods. It gives North Korea the tools it needs to be taken seriously and it gives China a tool for achieving its regional goals in the South China Sea and on the Korean Peninsula. This is a clear example of power generated through trade, particularly in China's case, as North

Korea is dependent on it and, more importantly, China keeps its strategic influence over the region because of that dependency.

Equally importantly, this chapter has illustrated the importance of conflict in some of the least stable regions of the world, with Syria being an excellent example of this. Russia's trade with Syria has clearly reflected its strategic interest, while the United Kingdom's trade with Saudi Arabia also reflects its foreign policy objectives. In the case of Syria, the involvement of greater powers is not just because they are protecting oil resources: they also have other, more strategic, interests.

As with the narrative elsewhere, the patterns that we have identified are not something new – it is just that our techniques for identifying them are new. Trade with Areas NES increased dramatically during the most rapid period of globalization. The growth rate of exports has slowed, but exports are still growing while imports have fallen back. This may indicate a shift in the use of Areas NES to being a trade repository, perhaps as a result of sanctions diversion, but at the very least it reinforces the fact that there is a link between trade and foreign policy that is not always overt.

Is this linked with the wars and regional conflicts that have characterized the patterns of violence over the last twenty years? Certainly, chapter 4 illustrated a strong and coherent link between trade, economic power and 'hard' power in its traditional sense. This chapter has given an indication of how that power translates into less transparent, more strategic interests. There does seem to be a link between political stability, economic growth and arms trade. The following chapter focuses on that link.

Chapter 6

Strategic trade and political instability: is there a link?

If the previous chapter demonstrated anything, it is that a considerable amount of trade is hidden and that this hidden trade is related to both national security and energy security. The countries that report their data best are those that are the most explicit about their trade with Areas NES. For example, not only does the United Kingdom rank top for the proportion of dual-use goods as a share of its total trade, at 29%, but it also traded $8.4 billion with Areas NES, all of which was recorded as commodities NES. In other words, the trade is concealed because it may be strategically important. For example, the Netherlands traded over $20 billion with all of the hidden partners – Areas NES, Bunkers, Special Categories and Free Zones – reflecting the importance of its role as a port in the oil supply chain.

It is highly improbable that the general public, or even senior policymakers, are aware of the existence of hidden trade. But if this hidden trade around the world is creating conflict because of the types of things that are traded, then it stands to reason that the public will know about the outcomes of these operations, not least because of the impact they have had on humanitarian crises and refugee flows around the world.

This chapter looks first at the relationships between arms trade, political stability, and per capita GDP (as an indicator of economic development). It finds that there is a positive relationship between GDP per capita and arms trade, which, on the basis of the previous chapters, can be attributed to the power of the biggest trading nations to supply arms around the world. It also finds that a country with low GDP per capita is nearly four times as likely to experience political instability as a country with high GDP per capita. Similarly, a country with year-on-year growth in arms imports over the globalization period is nearly five times as likely to experience political instability as a country that does not exhibit that same growth. It appears that the countries with the strongest soft power in economic terms are also those who have substantial exports of arms as well. In the words of a senior finance professional:

> There will always be trade in arms – it's good business. The key is to make sure we know where those guns are going and who the end-user is.

However, as a senior politician argued, 'let's be realistic, weapons will always be used – they are a means of conflict after all'.

Second, by using the case study of Saudi Arabia's trade with Yemen, we look at the potential role that arms trade has in fuelling proxy conflicts. The suggestion that arms trade can fuel political instability in poorer countries is hardly new or surprising. However, we return again to the idea that trade is now an explicit tool to achieve strategic objectives.

Internal conflict, GDP and trade

How helpful is trade data in understanding the link between internal conflict and arms trade? To establish this we undertook some more detailed analysis of these variables across the countries for which suitable data was available.

We measure political instability using casualty data from the Uppsala Conflict Data Program, which uses the georeferenced event data se[79]. This data set covers internal political violence between 1989 and 2015 and, as such, it excludes any cross-border violence, inter-state conflict and most (although not all[80]) deaths by terrorism. It is generally understood that the principal factors affecting political instability are frequent regime change and internal violence. However, studies using these variables often use ordinal data to reflect the intensity of the instability; this means the data can include subjective judgements. By assuming that higher levels of political instability will be reflected in higher casualties, this subjectivity is removed.

Table 1 groups 176 countries into four groups (44 cases per group) and then compares the Fragile States Index's stability rating with average casualty statistics for each country.[81]

Table 1. Political stability and states experiencing regular violence compared. *Source*: authors' analysis.

Level of stability	Number of states experiencing regular violence (%)
Very high political instability	38/44 (86.4)
High political instability	17/44 (38.6)
Low political instability	10/44 (22.7)
Very low political instability	2/44 (4.5)

'Regular violence' is defined as more than fifty deaths per annum occurring in over 25% of the years in the time period studied. The data shows that states ranking as highly politically unstable also experience a higher degree of political violence.

From this, we ran regression analysis on political stability as the dependent variable. We looked at this against two independent variables – GDP and arms trade – with the following results.

- With a p-value of 0.001 (indicating very high statistical significance), a country with low GDP per capita is 3.96 times more likely to experience political instability than a country with high GDP per capita.
- With a p-value of 0.0001, a country with arms imports that are growing by more than 40% year-on-year is 4.79 times more likely to experience political instability than a country with arms imports growth below that level.

At an individual country level what is striking is the fact that the majority of the 176 cases covered showed statistically significant positive or negative relationships with arms trade (at the 5% or 1% level). Ninety-eight of these show a statistically significant relationship with GDP. The results can be summarized as follows.

- The relationship between GDP and violent deaths suggests that lower GDP per capita causes higher deaths in 71 of the countries. In other words, for the majority of cases, low GDP per capita is a causal factor in driving higher levels of death.
- In 49 cases, the relationship between violent deaths and arms trade is positive: in other words, the higher the arms trade, the more violent deaths and political instability there is likely to be.

- There are 30 cases where arms trade is negatively correlated with deaths and political instability. On closer examination of the countries in this category – for example, the United States, Thailand, Nigeria and Mexico, which may at first seem like odd bedfellows – they are countries where the state has strong authority to use force against internal disturbance. Hence, the harder power embodied in the arms trade translates directly to the use of force to quell domestic conflict.

The interesting countries are those with the expected results: low GDP and high casualties, and volatile arms trade and high casualties. There are 41 of these cases. Their trade is volatile arguably for two reasons. First, because the country itself is poorer, meaning that data is badly reported and that formal (explicit) arms trade is less frequent than, perhaps, black market arms trade. Second, arms trade is lower because these are countries that are prone to unplanned violence. They are not all 'state-led' countries, and imports of arms may not be state sanctioned. Countries like Yemen, Chad, Rwanda, the Central African Republic and Libya are included in this group: they are all prone to conflict. All have contributed to global humanitarian and refugee crises.

Yemen is an excellent example of how conflict can be fuelled by the actions of other states. The humanitarian crisis has been developing there since 2015, when the conflict began. Earlier in this book we referred to Theresa May's April 2017 trip to Saudi Arabia, when she argued that the trade deals she had done with Saudi Arabia were in the United Kingdom's national and security interests. Similarly, President Trump's trade deal with Saudi Arabia was predominantly in arms and military equipment, again suggesting that there were strategic objectives in selling them.

Saudi Arabia does not report its trade in arms and ammunition with Yemen. Both countries have poor reporting and, as a result, we need to look at other countries' trade with Saudi Arabia. Figure 22 shows Saudi Arabia's trade with the world in this sector.

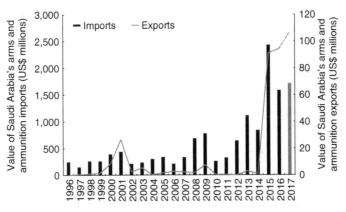

Figure 22. Value of Saudi Arabia's arms and ammunition trade, 1996–2017 (millions of US dollars). *Source*: Equant Analytics, 2017. *Note*: 2017 is estimated.

Two things are clear from the chart.

- There was a substantial increase in imports of arms between 2011 and 2013. These dates are broadly consistent with the Arab Spring.
- The most marked increase in both exports and imports is between 2014 and 2015: just before and at the start of the conflict with Yemen. Exports of arms continued to grow into 2016 and are projected to grow further in 2017. Although Saudi Arabia's imports of arms and ammunition look to have fallen back in 2016, the projections for 2017 again suggest an increase.

According to the Stockholm International Peace Research Institute, many arms deals include substantial intellectual property and knowledge transfer because they enable the partner in that deal to produce the weapons locally. Figure 21 in chapter 5 shows how important dual-use goods trade is in this context for trade between the United Kingdom and Saudi Arabia, for example.

Focusing just on the arms and ammunition trade itself is crucial because of the relationship between small arms and ammunition and insurgencies and political instability. The trade is hard to regulate, however. Although it falls within the UN Arms Trade Treaty (ATT) of 2014, the ATT requires the trade to be registered, but interestingly does not require it to be reported. Loans, leasing and gifts of arms are excluded from the treaty, and Saudi Arabia is not a signatory anyway. According to the UN, more than 80% of ammunition trade is excluded from reliable export data.[82] In other words, neither the suppliers nor the end users of arms and ammunition are reporting their usage or their trade.

Given this, it is instructive to look at countries where the trade *is* recorded: the United States and the United Kingdom are good examples here because both are signatories to the ATT, even though the United States has not yet ratified it.

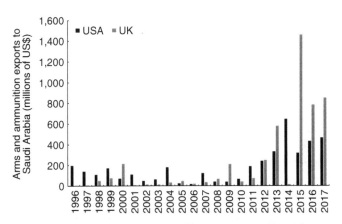

Figure 23. US and UK arms and ammunition trade with Saudi Arabia. *Source*: Equant Analytics, 2017.

Figure 23 speaks for itself. It shows a major increase in arms and ammunition exports from the United States to Saudi Arabia up to 2014. The United Kingdom's exports to Saudi Arabia increased to $1.5 billion between 2014 and 2015: more than twice the level of US arms exports. Both countries have increased their exports since 2011.

What is clear from this is that the arms and ammunition trade with Saudi Arabia is fuelling conflict in the region, in both Syria and Yemen. But what is equally clear is that the reporting is poor and that the size and scale of arms and ammunition trade is hard to capture fully. The United States, for example, has allegedly argued that ammunition is hard to include in regulations because bullets are hard to track.[83] However, the important point here is that while used weapons and weapons parts can be passed over borders, only *unused* ammunition can be traded – with terrible consequences.

Summary

Arms trade is clearly linked to political instability. It is better than GDP at predicting violence and political instability in our global sample. It is also a core driver of instability in 41 countries that could do with it least: that is, those that are already poor and conflict prone. It has created a refugee crisis in Europe and across the world as individuals seek to escape conflict zones. Some of these conflicts may well be proxy wars fought through intermediaries on behalf of bigger powers to ensure energy supplies. Others may be the result of internal power struggles with religious or ethnic foundations. Whatever they are, they are the clashes of civilizations[84] – the conflicts between groups, rather than the wars between nations – that are identified with the global era.

Syria was excluded from our analysis partly on data grounds and partly because the number of deaths was so high that it was too extreme and distorted the results. Yet it is that conflict that created the European refugee crisis that in the end dominated the Brexit vote. Europe's response in 2015 was, for the first time since World War II, nationalistic. As one high-ranking French official argued at an event in October 2015, 'the Germans destroyed Schengen: we know that if we can't close borders we will have a terrorist crisis on our hands'. Four weeks later the Paris attacks happened. Yet Germany's response to the refugee crisis has been entirely in line with its constitution: its national interests could be served by bringing in more skills to address its skills shortage, and its foreign policy role was a humanitarian one only.

The confusion across Europe and the subsequent attacks in Paris and Brussels – followed, of course, by attacks in Berlin, London and Stockholm – have not helped the European public to think clearly about the distinction between genuine refugees and terrorism. Indeed, the media and politicians themselves have stoked up anti-immigration sentiment that has conflated immigration and the refugee crisis in the collective moral panic referred to at the beginning of chapter 5. The consequent nationalism and economic nationalism have done nothing to further the cause of free trade – but then trade is itself partly responsible.

But more importantly, what this chapter has demonstrated is that strategic trade not only applies to security-related trade that is 'hidden' in the 'national interest'. It is also the case that arms trade occurs because there is strategic interest in fighting 'arm's-length' wars using trade as a vehicle. Not simply because, in the words of one interviewee, 'there is money to be made'.

This is a huge challenge for civil society: trade in arms and ammunition is in direct conflict with a requirement for foreign policy to have solid foundations in humanitarian support and economic development. The arms embargo on Yemen was extended in spring 2017, but it is clearly having a limited effect. The ongoing conflict being fought on its territory has had devastating civilian consequences, highlighting the human cost of the arms trade.

Chapter 7

Policy lessons: the great rebalancing of politics and economics

Particularly the change in Washington puts the European Union in a difficult situation; with the new administration seeming to put into question the last 70 years of American foreign policy.

— *Donald Tusk*[85]

At the beginning of this book we defined weaponization as 'the transformation of a benign instrument into a means of aggression'. We argued that, through rhetoric, trade has been weaponized, both literally and figuratively: first through the arms trade and second as a coercive tool of state strategy. It seems to have reached the point where the mutually beneficial economic aspects of trade have been replaced by political agendas. In several states trade has become something nationalistic and adversarial; partners are 'enemies', deals are 'unfair' and vital to 'national security'. In short, the balance between politics and economics that trade has struck historically has tipped dangerously in favour of politics.

Governments in the United States and United Kingdom need to be aware of this historical juncture we now find ourselves at. If this weaponization of trade is not addressed, the idea that it is something *destructive* is in danger of becoming entrenched and the *constructive* economic aspects may be lost.

As a case in point, as this book was going to press it was announced that Donald Trump was planning to ease export rules for US arms.[86] This reinforced the perception, outlined in an open letter by Donald Tusk in January 2017, that the institutions and structures of the post-World War II order are being undermined, indeed dismantled, in the name of economic nationalism.

Worryingly, it does not currently appear that there is an appetite among key policymakers to engage in a renewed multilateralist agenda that addresses the concerns that have been highlighted through populism. And yet this is what is sorely needed.

In short, policymakers cannot avoid the fact that business today is global and that this requires a degree of multilateralism. Aggressive rhetoric can make multilateralism more difficult by inhibiting investment decisions or creating a sense of isolationism. After all, putting 'America first' necessarily places its partners second.

Tackling weaponization through economics

> The world isn't going to be any less complicated. You can't dis-invent technology or liberal democracy or cross-border movements of capital. But more importantly, you can't create something less bad through populism.

— Senior risk analyst

There are three potential policy areas where it may be possible to rebalance trade discourse back to economics from its current precarious domination of politics. The first is to address the root causes of populism. Politicians in the United Kingdom and the United States should acknowledge that populism is creating political instability for themselves: the UK general election in June 2017 and President Trump's low approval ratings are testimony to this. In other words, using a populist tone is self-defeating. Weaponized language is a dangerous tool in that it hardens populism. What people need is information: they need to see that they benefit from globalization more than they benefit from nationalism. Worse still, weaponized language is damaging in diplomatic terms: calling a state 'very bad', even if this is playing well to a domestic audience, does nothing to promote multilateralism.

In the current climate, this is an increasingly hard circle to square, but insofar as exporting businesses create jobs locally, trade finance for SMEs is a good place to start. During 2016 there was a 97% drop in trade finance through US Exim, the US-government-backed export credit agency.[87] This corresponded with substantial drops in trade finance in Japan, Germany and South Korea driven by generally weak trade and a shift in the way in which exports are financed from traditional letters of credit to open account trade finance. However, US Exim has been technically liquidated since April 2015, when its license expired. While the current administration sees it as part of the trade toolbox, its status still remains unclear. This confusion needs to be addressed at the earliest opportunity.

In contrast to what is happening in the United States, UK Export Finance increased its level of financing by nearly 200% as a result of policies to support exporters after Brexit. This increase was from a relatively low base, however, and there is much ongoing work to increase awareness about overseas markets among the small business community and to demonstrate how business can be acquired in these markets. Given the uncertainties around both the nature of the United Kingdom's trade deal with Europe after Brexit and the nature of the transition phase, the task of UK Export Finance may be made difficult by weak demand for its product among the small business community.

The 'trade not aid' mantra of the early years of globalization is helpful in widening its benefits in terms of economic development. For example, the sustainable development goals include building the capacity of communities in emerging markets to be self-sufficient through the activity of SMEs. Across the world, as we saw in the previous chapter, there is a $1.6 trillion trade finance gap, and this gap hits emerging Asian markets hardest.[88] This requires regulatory systems to take into account the need for sustainable development as well as the need, quite rightly, for businesses to know who their clients are and avoid money laundering. The United States should recommit itself to the US–Africa trade relationship, while the United Kingdom's Department for International Development's focus on the 'trade not aid' agenda should be redoubled.

Tackling weaponization through finance and regulation

The second key policy area to address is the drop in trade itself. The current withdrawal from multilateral agreements by both the United Kingdom and the United States raises an important question: who takes overall responsibility for dispute resolution, regulatory equivalence and compliance in bilateral trade relations? Ironically, by withdrawing from the Trans-Atlantic Trade and Investment Partnership (TTIP) and the Trans-Pacific Partnership, the United States has potentially weakened its global regulatory reach, particularly in Asia but potentially in Europe too. The evolving laws attached to both of those arrangements would, arguably, have placed the ultimate arbitration with US regulators.

At present, US regulators hold sway because of their power over trade finance: for example, although the sanctions against Iran have loosened in the United Kingdom and Europe, it is still difficult for businesses to raise finance to trade there because any involvement at any stage by US banks, including pricing the deal in US dollars, cannot get through US regulators. Disputes are likely to increase as the post-Brexit dust settles through any transition period, and it is unclear which regulator will take precedence or where disputes will be resolved. This presents exporters and their financiers with huge uncertainty, with obvious consequences for trade growth in the near term. Resolving these uncertainties must be a priority.

Indeed, regulators have been at the heart of the slow-down in trade in recent years. It cannot be seen as entirely coincidental that trade has slowed markedly since HSBC was first fined $1.9 billion in 2012 over money laundering.[89] Standard Chartered Bank was subsequently fined $340 million in 2012 for breaching sanctions imposed on Iran,[90] and between 2015 and midway through 2017 some $12.6 billion in fines for sanctions non-compliance were levied. Fines of an estimated $4 billion between February 2016 and January 2017 for non-compliance were additionally imposed on global banks.[91] Alongside this, Basel III capital ratio compliance issues have continued to apply to smaller trade finance deals, despite the contention of the International Chamber of Commerce's

Banking Commission that trade finance transactions are less risky.[92] Low yields because of low interest rates have also had an effect on the trade finance market.

All of this has had the effect of making banks themselves look for higher returns from the largest clients that they know best. The various compliance and regulatory concerns have made it expensive for banks to do deals with smaller companies in less stable parts of the world. Trade finance and trade are closely associated with each other: WTO estimates suggest that 80–90% of the value of world trade is accounted for by some form of trade finance, with bank intermediate trade finance being some 35% of that. It would be disingenuous to blame the slowdown in trade entirely on a drop in trade finance induced by regulation and compliance issues, but the fact that both trade and trade finance have dropped simultaneously cannot be ignored. This is not least because trade finance is something that can be supported by policy measures by entities such as US Exim and UK Export Finance. Regulation needs to be smart rather than tight – targeted at preventing certain trade, like ammunition, without preventing trade that helps sustainable development, like food, for example.

Rediscovering trade's balance with politics

This leads to the final – and arguably the most important – area in which policy can make a difference. We have argued that trade is being weaponized: it has moved from being an objective of foreign policy in the earliest phases of globalization through to being an explicit tool for foreign policy to gain power and influence.

What is important now is that trade is being used as a tool of state strategy using techniques that have never been used before. This is enabled through the interconnectedness of the world's media; policy can be announced through tweets and chance comments can be interpreted as policy as they are sent viral. At best, this is irresponsible.

But more irresponsible is the fact that arms and ammunition trade can still be used as a means for more powerful nations to wield influence indirectly: somebody else's war becomes a vehicle for achieving power or influence. We have observed this happening in the Middle East with long-lasting damage to political stability and significant human cost.

The fines imposed by US and UK regulators on banks for sanctions or AML noncompliance would suggest that it is the banking sector that is to blame. Yet it is also clear that the controls to prevent weapons from reaching conflict zones are weak. Indeed, the United States is now explicitly trying to weaken and dismantle these structures further to support US arms trade while ensuring that the regulators have tough powers to impose substantial fines against banks. This is not to say that banks should not be fined for any noncompliance with sanctions or AML regulations – they should be. But it does point to a paradox in policy that supports arms trade on the one hand while fining banks for financing it on the other.

It is here where there is the greatest need to redress the balance between the battlefield and the boardroom. Why? Because the rules of engagement between the politics and the economics of trade are not clear. It is here where the politicians have the greatest power to 'disarm' trade, literally and figuratively, for the benefit of all.

Summary

Any policy recommendation will sound trite, since the issues at stake concern the type of world we want to live in. It would be too easy to say that this requires global leadership, for example. There is a crisis of democratic legitimacy alongside an increased need to think about the consequences of strategic trade as a tool of coercion and influence. It needs responsibility and understanding, not leadership as such, and that is a much bigger ask. Regulatory frameworks that support trade finance to smaller businesses acknowledge the role of diplomacy and foreign policy in supporting trade. This is necessary, but not sufficient. In the end, a greater awareness of the importance of trade and globalization is critical – and that relies on politicians around the world realizing that the public are unclear as to how globalization matters. It is in the interests of every nation that this is explained, and it is the responsibility of governments to have the humility to do just that in the interests of enhancing, rather than destroying, the institutions that have supported economic growth and peace in the post-war period.

Post-war economic critiques of the so-called Anglo-Saxon model have focused on its inherent short-termism; what we are witnessing now is a product of short-term, tactical thinking in the United States and the United Kingdom. The response to public expressions of uncertainty has been to invoke the spirit of nationalism and protectionism. The result has engendered yet more confusion, not least because neither Brexit nor 'Make America Great Again' solve the long-term problems of migration, terrorism or rising inequality.

To repeat, there is no easy policy solution, and understanding domestic populism is at least as much about addressing issues around real pay growth, inequality and domestic economic and personal security as it is about global influence. However, the nations that will benefit from the current global transition are those that are playing the long game with adaptable economic and political strategies.

The United States, through its current economic and political isolationism, is in danger of sacrificing global influence by allowing short-term tactics to dominate its thinking. This is a tension that is at the heart of the American system. That tension may yet be its undoing if the current presidential rhetoric cannot be tamed. The United States's, indeed the world's, institutional structures are being damaged by both rhetoric and action.

In contrast, the United Kingdom has always had short-termism ingrained in its economic and political system, but through trade and the legacy of empire it has always been able to punch above its weight. The danger is that, as Brexit and a more nationalistic undercurrent begin to dominate, the country will lose an element of the influence it once had.

The United States and the United Kingdom are where they are because of short-term military and economic tactics that have prioritized short-term rhetorical influence in an attempt to mollify domestic populism. This has allowed a counterproductive, weaponized narrative around trade to emerge. It is in their interests, as well as the interests of the world, that longer-term strategic thinking, domestically as well as internationally, is put at the forefront of politics as soon as possible in both countries. This means that belligerent language should be avoided at all costs. We need to return to a point where trade strikes a balance between politics and economics once again.

Chapter 8

Conclusions: strategic trade wars?

One of the most difficult things about writing a book that combines disciplines, data analysis and current news is that the core messages become blurred. But we hope that our focus has nevertheless remained clear. We have tried to demonstrate how the process of globalization between 1998 and 2014 created an identity void for individuals who saw themselves as national rather than global citizens. Similarly, the relative failure of military engagements in the likes of Afghanistan and Iraq has demonstrated the limitations of national strategic power, not least because insurgencies and localized wars create long-term strategic problems beyond pure conflict – the wave of immigration globally being perhaps the most pressing.

These two problems combined have resulted in the populist backlash that was apparent in the form of the Brexit vote in the United Kingdom in June 2016, the election of President Trump, and respective elections in France and the Netherlands. We are referring here to the wave of populism discussed in chapter 2. It has pitched individuals against each other in the quest for a meaningful identity and given rise to many of the conflicts, in soft- and hard-power terms, that we have seen become more acute since the financial crisis. We have argued that populism has been a key feature of elections and referenda in Europe and the United States since 2014. It is a product of the latest stage of globalization and has created the sense of economic nationalism that has started to underpin policy, even in countries such as Germany and France that are not explicitly nationalistic. In contrast to the period of globalization from the end of the Cold War to the end of 2014, what is unfolding now is political. It can be differentiated from previous stages because economic nationalism dominates the rhetoric and strategic trade directs the foreign policy.

There is clearly much we do not know about this emerging era – almost by definition. It is relatively new and its protagonists have populist agendas that may vary according to political events. The fact that Marine Le Pen was defeated in the French presidential election and that Theresa May did not win the UK election outright that she called for 8 June 2017 could perhaps be interpreted as a move away from the populism that has been so obvious in the public discourse. But populism has already been highly disruptive and has the potential to be highly disruptive again in the future: both to the structure of multilateral 'free' trade and to the way in which countries settle conflicts.

The defining feature of the evolving political stage of globalization is what we have called 'strategic trade'. That is, trade that serves the purpose of furthering strategic influence, both nationally and internationally. We argue that this trade is highly concentrated in strategic sectors such as arms, electronics, communications technologies, aerospace, oil and gas. These are also sectors in which dual-use goods are found. These, by definition, can be used for military or civilian purposes, but, as we argued, the definition of what is military and what is civilian is no longer clear. For example, cyber defence systems are not necessarily built by individuals with formal military training and yet they provide 'protection' against cyber attacks. This means that the scale of dual-use goods trade is itself a good proxy for the strategic intent of a country.

Similarly, 'strategic trade' facilitates indirect wars and has become the preferred means of engagement as a result of Western failures in recent conflicts. Trade is used as a vehicle for coercion: either through orthodox trade wars (protectionism and sanctions) or through targeted exports in specific sectors to specific countries. This does not directly involve conflict for the exporting nation, but bears the hallmarks of war in the definitional sense in that it is the continuation of policy by other means.

There are four aspects to the narrative in this book. First, we showed the importance of the nation state and the balance between soft and hard power through trade. There has always been a link between trade and power since industrialization began in the 1800s. It gave rise to empire and imperialism in Europe and, in the interest of protecting national economic interests through trade, it also gave rise to wars and conflict. For example, the system of post-war multilateral trade and military agreements enshrined in the Treaty of Rome after World War II were designed to prevent physical conflict between European nations through the shared interests of economic stability and growth.

This link between politics and economics became more entrenched throughout the period of globalization after the Cold War. The character of trade and war changed as a result of greater international connectedness and as a result of new technologies. Globalization, it was argued, is full of contradictions, and these are evident both in the way in which trade has shifted the balance of power from industrial war to insurgencies and, equally, in strategic trade wars bound up with protecting historical national interests. During this period, large standing armies have been deemed surplus to requirements in the face of so-called new threats, but this does not mean that there is no conflict, just that the chosen means of influencing those conflicts has changed.

The nation state, by which we mean its institutions, remains the dominant force in all of this. We looked at how the hard and soft power between countries balances out and we showed that only Germany, Japan and South Korea have more soft power than hard power (Germany and Japan for constitutional reasons). But we noted the very high correlation between arms trade growth and growth in dual-use goods, which suggested a stronger link between trade and strategic intent by nation states.

The second strand of our narrative related to our argument that this strategic intent is evident in the ways in which trade is hidden by countries. This is measured in the first instance through dual-use goods, and in the second through the amounts of trade that are obscured in locations like 'Areas not elsewhere specified' and 'Bunkers' or in goods that are not defined, like 'commodities not elsewhere specified'. We showed how this trade may be used as a means of diverting trade during sanctions or to provide goods to areas where the interests of companies supplying those goods are best protected.

Third, military trade and trade in commodities not elsewhere specified are highly correlated, and the fact that there is trade that is unaccounted for in concealed sectors gives rise to the inference that this trade is both protecting energy supplies and being used to provide resources to fight proxy wars. In other words, trade can be used as the chosen means for directing war and conflict.

We used to speak of trade wars fought through sanctions and protectionist tariffs and taxes. But we argue that these are relatively weak tools, not least because of likely reciprocation on a bilateral basis. Instead, we argue that we should be speaking of trade as a key component of military strategy given that it seems to be increasingly associated with war: directly through the arms trade and indirectly through dual-use goods and 'hidden' trade. The disturbing empirical evidence for this was provided by an analysis covering 176 countries that showed that countries with low GDP and high growth in arms imports were more likely to be politically unstable. In 41 countries, among which are some of the poorest and least stable in the world, arms trade and low GDP can be used as a predictor of political instability. This indicates a worrying link between the hidden trade we have uncovered and internal conflict, with the resultant refugee crisis that the world has witnessed over the past two years.

Finally, our analysis is based on the observation that trade has become increasingly weaponized. There is little comfort in this. But this weaponization can be understood on two levels: first as a by-product of the globalization process itself, and second in terms of its use as a strategic tool for coercion and foreign policy influence. In search of political legitimacy, politicians have sought to reconnect with a public that has become increasingly frustrated at the loss of control and influence it has experienced. Globalization has made everyone a global citizen without giving them a sense of what that means. The result is the collapse of social structures, leaving an identity and behavioural void.

This void has been filled with nationalist rhetoric. In other words, we have gone full circle: back to the national identities that preceded the end of the Cold War. On one level, this can be positive if those identities are used to promote diplomacy, integrity, liberty and freedom within a world that is characterized by free trade and movement of people. But the danger at present is that that void will not be filled through soft power rhetoric. Politicians have found both legitimacy from their voters and a more cogent articulation of their international positions through nationalist rhetoric. The process of digitization and global connectedness cannot be undone. The results of recent European elections perhaps suggest that nationalism is not what the public wants after all.

But the fact is that digital media has been harnessed with nationalist sentiment, painting a worrying picture of what the world might look like in ten years' time if this is allowed to continue. It is always dangerous to invoke the spirit of war, but especially so if trade war and economic nationalism lead to a resurgence of more conventional nationalism. In the words of one former diplomat:

> It's easy for a politician if it isn't you or your country who is to blame: look at Putin, or indeed Trump – their domestic power is based on a narrative that says, 'everyone is against us, but I can protect you'.

Where does it all end?

We are ever optimists. The compelling attractions of free trade for business are clear, and it is businesses that trade, not governments. Governments simply set the frameworks, and their policy tools are as limited in trade wars as they are in more conventional forms of war: the danger of retaliation is too great. That does not mean governments will not play an important role. Strategic trade says that trade is a means of coercion forcing others into agreement or alignment. In other words, whether as an attempt at realpolitik (the politics of the practical in the case of Brexit) or as outright belligerence (the politics of the Korean peninsula), trade's role is about achieving influence.

Europe is a good example of the realpolitik of the strategic trade spectrum. The negotiations around the United Kingdom's exit from the EU will not be straightforward, despite any pretence that they may be. The United Kingdom initially relied on a conciliatory Europe led by a Germany that was genuinely saddened by the loss of its like-minded Anglo-Saxon ally, making it more likely to drive the bloc towards compromise. The G7 and NATO summits at the end of May, and the inauguration of President Macron, changed that. Europe found a new assertiveness on the global stage. This was articulated by Chancellor Merkel in her Munich speech at the end of May 2017: she argued that the United States and the

United Kingdom could no longer be relied upon and that Europe must find its own voice to promote its own interests. In the words of one former senior EU diplomat: 'Europe itself is now pushing its own identity. It has to.' While much of the rhetorical anger in Merkel's speech was attributed to electioneering, it served as a wake-up call to the United Kingdom. Europe will have its own strategic interests, not least because of Germany's influence when it starts the negotiations. Both the trade and the influence aspects of Germany's policy in the run up to its election were captured in a comment from a senior German politician: 'We have been very bad at strategy generally. But we are becoming very strategic about trade.'

Trade is political and this makes it strategic: that is, something that can be used as a tool to promote national or regional interests in economic or foreign policy terms. In this, EU negotiators will be keen to protect Europe's economic and energy security as well as its increasingly focused foreign policy interests.

An illustrative example

The EU's top ten export and import trade flows with the United Kingdom by sector are automotives, machinery (including computers), pharmaceuticals, electrical equipment and oil and gas (figure 24). The top fifteen trade flows by sector add optical, photographic and medical equipment, plastics and aerospace. These are not just the top trade sectors for the EU as a whole: they are also among the top sectors for Germany, France, the Netherlands, Italy, Belgium and, naturally, the United Kingdom.

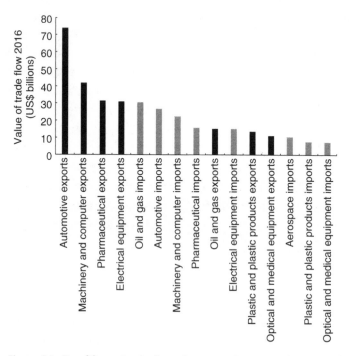

Figure 24. Top fifteen trade flows by sector between the EU and the United Kingdom (exports and imports, 2016, billions of US dollars). *Source*: Equant Analytics, 2017.

Given that Europe exports some 85% more to the United Kingdom than it imports from the country, it has been assumed that the cards are stacked in the United Kingdom's favour. However, trade 'wars' are reciprocal: one side imposes tougher arrangements and the other retaliates. As these are the top sectors for the United Kingdom as well, and as Europe is the United Kingdom's largest export destination for each of these sectors, it will be important to bear in mind that the symbiotic relationship in these sectors is because of Europe-wide supply chains. Everyone will lose without some compromise.

The second thing to note is just how concentrated this trade is. The top ten flows account for 53% of Europe's trade with the United Kingdom. Add in plastics, optical and medical equipment and aerospace (the eleventh and twelfth largest flows, and in the top five for Germany, France and Italy) and the top flows account for over 60% of Europe's trade with the United Kingdom (figure 25).

Again, the dominance of exports to the United Kingdom is clear: the top four sectors are all exports to the United Kingdom and constitute over 31% of Europe's trade with the country. The importance of Europe-wide supply chains is again critical, however. The United Kingdom is a large export market for German cars and automotive components, but this is because it is a major location within Europe for the *manufacture* of German cars. While this may make it seem like Germany is more dependent on the United Kingdom than the other way round, the United Kingdom's exports of cars to the United States and China have grown at annualized rates of 9% and 13%, respectively, over the past five years. This is not all attributable to German manufacturers, but there is no doubt that this has had an influence.

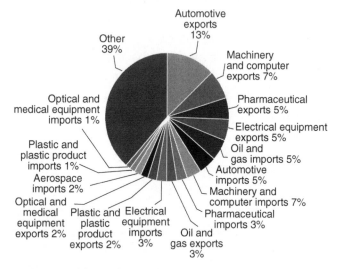

Figure 25. Share of EU trade with the United Kingdom: top fifteen sectors, 2016 (%). *Source*: Equant Analytics, 2017.

Finally, EU trade has been highly correlated with the value of the euro since its inception in 1998, as illustrated in figure 26. This highlights that the euro remains a currency whose value is rooted in the real economy of the bloc rather than being speculative. The euro is the world's second largest trade finance currency and its position and strength can therefore be seen as a function of the strength of Europe's trade. This is a quite distinct function for the euro and explains why Germany in particular has been keen to hold the Eurozone together: the euro's economic importance is in trade, and as supply chains develop across the region, this becomes more rather than less important. Just as is the case for Europe, a stable euro ensures that prices within the United Kingdom's supply chains, into which the country's businesses are woven, are also stable.

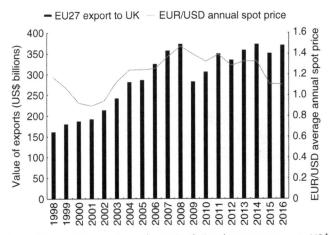

Figure 26. EU 27 exports to the United Kingdom versus euro–US$ spot price, 1998–2016. *Source*: Equant Analytics, 2017.

All of this shows just how important these strategic sectors are, both for the United Kingdom and for Europe. While the process of negotiations through to the

United Kingdom's formal exit from the EU may be painful, the strategic imperative for both sides to come to an agreement is quite clear from the above. In the end, we have to hope that strategic interests outweigh rhetorical ones as these are both economic and related to security.

We asked our interviewees if they felt that we were at a historical juncture. All of them felt that this was an important, if not defining, period in history, with attendant dangers as well. However, in the words of one senior German diplomat:

> Every era in history has its special challenges and now it is the dual threats of globalization *and* disintegration. These are forces that don't stop at borders – no one country can do this alone so the developed world, and the EU in particular, needs to hold together. We can't pull up the drawbridge and ignore the 'others' next door. We know there are dangers but we have to see this moment as a catharsis.

A trade lawyer argued similarly: 'The forces of economic nationalism will run into countervailing pressures. It won't last, but it may shift the world order.' In the light of the aftermath of the UK election, this last point seems particularly prescient.

Our analysis of soft and hard power suggested two key shifts that might emerge. The first is towards trade as a predictor of influence and responsibility. Many interviewees argued that this shift within Europe was likely to awaken Germany to its global responsibilities. One comment was that Germany would be provoked into using more belligerent language or even into using words that do not sit well with its history – words such as 'leadership'. But all felt that Germany should not 'rise to the bait': that it was a global trading power and that this gave it a responsibility to protect trade in all its forms but also, alongside this, to take up a greater security role. Its strategic influence is because it has soft power, which is no less coercive but relies on different means for that coercion.

The second shift was in the role that strategic trade directly plays in gaining power. Here interviewees felt that China would be the main beneficiary. 'China's trade power is immense, giving it huge soft power,' argued one, 'but don't forget it also has a huge military. That counts for something even if it doesn't use it.' Generally, interviewees felt that China could play a long game. Its strategic regional interests are locked into its trade interests, and because of this it has the power to lead rather than follow the United States. China does not need to play a military card: by championing trade at a WTO level, it has arguably replaced the influence that the United States once had with its own. In the end, China's strategic gain will be entirely through its trade influence – in international organizations such as the Asian Infrastructure and Investment Bank and in its own infrastructural strategic relationships, such as the $900 billion Belt and Road infrastructure initiative, in which President Xi describes China as a 'peace-loving explorer set on transforming the world with treasure-laden galleys not warships, guns or swords'.[93]

What is critical here is that trade is clearly more important than simply as an economic concept; and trade wars are more than just protectionism. Strategic trade is itself an important concept to understand, not just in a domestic context, but also for understanding how countries build their strategic influence and power abroad. As so many of our trade and political relationships in Europe, in the United States and across the world are called into doubt by current rhetoric, this concept is likely to become more, rather than less, important.

Yet the election result in the United Kingdom arguably demonstrated the weakness of the weaponized language approach. The electorate had moved on to other issues, notably broader concerns about the impact of austerity (such as inequality, living standards and low real wage growth) rather than nationalism. Theresa May was unable to reconnect with voters through nationalist, even war-like, rhetoric. Voters do not want war although – in the words of a senior German politician – 'UK voters seem better at telling everyone what they don't want than what they do want'. But the electorate does want the political process to reflect their pain. In manifestly sticking to the same militarized rhetoric, Theresa May distanced herself further from them and proved that weaponized language is dangerous – not least because it failed to guarantee electoral success!

But what this does is point out just how carefully policymakers must address both the current political instabilities and the strategic trade that we have identified here. Above all, weaponized language is risky and illustrates one aspect of our interviews that emerged consistently: the need for politicians to take some responsibility for both the rise of populism and its aftermath. Some called this the need for global leadership; the Germans among the interviewees called it responsibility, but in the end it meant the same thing: this is a crisis moment in history and any loose language has the potential to do lasting damage. Many wanted to see lasting change after the Brexit vote, the election of Donald Trump and even after the UK general election. Our interviewees argued that the responsibility now lies with politicians to explain why globalization is important; and more critically, since it is not self-evident, how it benefits people economically, socially and culturally. However weak this sounds, the world cannot afford for trade itself to be weaponized.

Protectionism and economic nationalism are not the answer either. Instead, as our interviewees identified, trade needs better regulatory structures. Regulatory improvements should ensure that the strictures of capital requirements and compliance conditions attached to trade finance are configured in a way that ensures that access to finance is not a barrier to trade, particularly for export-oriented small and medium-sized enterprises (SMEs) in emerging economies. The International Chamber of Commerce estimates that there is a $1.6 trillion finance gap for SMEs, which is something that can be addressed through effective credit insurance, through a better understanding of the risks of trade and trade finance, and through better mechanisms for dispute resolution.

One final thought: trade is strategic, and strategic trade, as we have defined it here, is a key part of achieving national power and influence. The rhetoric used by some politicians suggests that they are not treating this aspect of trade with the seriousness it deserves. It is the language that is risky, not necessarily the national interest embodied in strategic trade itself. Politicians, diplomats, negotiators and businesses alike would do well to recognize that national interest also means things like energy security. Perhaps if the strategic aspects of trade were better understood and articulated, those who speak in weaponized terms about trade would begin to show some humility.

Appendix

Methodology

General observation on the data source

The quantitative research for this book is based predominantly on the Equant Analytics Ltd proprietorial data set. This data set covers 200 countries and 12,800 products and sectors, as well as all the accompanying trade flows. The data is drawn from the UN's Comtrade data set, which is the official record of all customs and excise submissions to the United Nations. As such, it is a comprehensive and global data source. All values are presented in US dollars and we have stuck to that protocol.

Equant Analytics Ltd's data is different to other data in that it makes imports and exports equal across the world. In other words, the United Kingdom's trade with Germany will be identical to Germany's trade with the United Kingdom, where in the raw data there may be discrepancies. In the case of Germany and the United Kingdom, there is only a marginal difference (less than 5%), so the algorithms take the average of the two data sources. However, in the case of two countries with poorer reporting standards – South Africa and China, say – the discrepancy is much larger, although still less than 50%. In these cases the average flow is weighted towards the historically better-reported flow or country. For cases where the discrepancy is more than 50%, the algorithms take the data of the better-reporting country, and where data is missing altogether for one country (e.g. in many African countries for later years), the data that exists in the mirrored flow is taken.

This reconstructs data globally and fills gaps in the data that are evident when looking at more unusual trade routes and flows on Comtrade. The method is particularly relevant for establishing trade flows for the Middle East, North Africa and Sub-Saharan Africa, but it also applies equally well to the trade partners Areas NES, Bunkers, Free Zones and Special Categories, where values do not exist on Comtrade.

Chapter 4

Chapter 4's methodology is based on a ranking of the observable trade patterns of the G20 countries. These are

- world export ranking (by size of exports in US dollars),
- trade openness (total trade as a share of a country's GDP),

- correlation of arms trade to GDP, and
- percentage of country trade taken by dual-use goods.

The first and second items above are taken as being measures of soft power. The third and fourth are taken as being measures of hard power. Each of the G20 nations is ranked on a scale of 1–20 (with no weighting for the underlying absolute value). The unweighted average is taken to give a score between 1 and 20. Scores of 1–3.99 are classified as 'soft power', putting the associated country in the top left-hand corner of the quadrant. Scores of 4–7.99 are taken as 'hard power' and these countries are grouped in the top right-hand corner of the quadrant. Scores of 8–11.99 are taken as 'soft–hard', with the relevant countries being grouped into the bottom left-hand corner of the quadrant. And scores above 12 are taken as 'hard–soft', with countries grouped into the bottom right-hand corner of the quadrant. 'Soft' power and 'hard' power refer here to the prevalence or otherwise of traded goods that are directly associated with a more coercive foreign policy. A country can thus have strong, economically oriented foreign policy (such as in Germany) but there might be a limited connection between its trade and 'strategic intent' exhibited in its foreign policy.

An improvement on this method would be given by including some of the economies outside the G20, such as Hong Kong and Singapore in Asia and Denmark, Norway and Sweden in Europe.

Endnotes

1. C. von Clausewitz. 2008. *On War* (edited and translated by M. Howard and P. Paret), paperback edition, p. 13. Oxford University Press.

2. von Clausewitz (2008, p. 74).

3. B. Liddell Hart. 1967. *Strategy: The Indirect Approach,* pp. 333–335. London: Faber and Faber.

4. C. S. Gray. 2016. *Strategy and Politics*, p. 11. Oxford: Routledge.

5. P. Krugman (ed.). 1986. *Strategic Trade Policy and the New International Economics.* Cambridge, MA: MIT Press.

6. Goodhart's law, named after Charles Goodhart, states that when a measure becomes a target it ceases to be a good measure.

7. W. S. Lind, J. F. Schmitt and G. I. Wilson. 2001. Fourth generation warfare: another look. *Marine Corps Gazette* 85(11):69–71.

8. B. Allemby and J. Garreau. 2017. Weaponized narrative is the new battlespace. Defense One blog (http://bit.ly/2iRZeUe).

9. T. Friedman. 2007. *The World Is Flat: The Globalised World in the 21st Century,* 2nd edition. London: Penguin.

10. D. Coyle. 1999. *The Weightless World.* Cambridge, MA: MIT Press.

11. M. Kaldor. 1999. *New and Old Wars: Organised Violence in a Global Era.* Cambridge: Polity Press.

12. M. Wolf. 2017. Donald Trump and the surrendering of US leadership. *Financial Times,* 30 May (http://on.ft.com/2qyhmGe).

13. Office of the Press Secretary. 2017. Presidential Executive Order on Buy American and Hire American, 18 April (http://bit.ly/2pB59U1).

14. UK government website: 'Exporting is great' (www.export.great.gov.uk).

15. Reuters. 2017. 'I will protect you.' Marine Le Pen vows to end all immigration to France if elected president. *The Telegraph*, 18 April (http://bit.ly/2p1J0Nq).

16. D. Goodhart. 2017. *The Road to Somewhere: The Populist Revolt and the Future of Politics.* London: C. Hurst and Co.

17. The nickname given to UK 'remain' voters in social and tabloid media.

18. A. Marr. 2017. Anywheres vs somewheres: the split that made Brexit inevitable. *New Statesman*, 17 March (http://bit.ly/2mEbAQQ).

19. S. King. 2017. *Grave New World.* Newhaven, CT: Yale University Press.

20. This is a point also made in R. Findlay and K. H. O'Rourke. 2007. *Power and Plenty: Trade, War and the World Economy in the Second Millennium.* Princeton University Press.

21. R. Baldwin. 2016. *The Great Convergence: Information Technology and the New Globalization.* Cambridge, MA: Harvard University Press.

22. A. Hirschman. 1945 (reprinted 2006). *National Power and the Structure of Foreign Trade.* Oakland, CA: University of California Press.

23. E. Gellner. 1983. *Nations and Nationalism.* Ithaca, NY: Cornell University Press.

24. Hirschman (1945).

25. Hirschman (1945).

26. E. Luce. 2017. *The Retreat of Western Liberalism.* London: Little Brown.

27. M. Kaldor. 1999. *New and Old Wars: Organised Violence in a Global Era.* Stanford University Press.

28. F. Fukuyama. 1992 (reprinted 2012). *The End of History and the Last Man.* London: Penguin Books.

29. *The Economist.* 2017. The retreat of the global company. *The Economist*, 28 January, pp. 19–22 (http://econ.st/2ykPNo3).

30. A. Beesley and S. Donnan. 2017. Brussels vows to retaliate over US steel tariffs threat. *Financial Times*, 26 June (http://on.ft.com/2u9yKmk).

31. International Monetary Fund. 2017. World economic outlook, April 2017: gaining momentum? Report (http://bit.ly/2hdEYwn).

32. J. Manyika, J. Bughin, S. Lund, O. Nottebohm, D. Poulter, S. Jauch and S. Ramaswamy. 2014. Global flows in a digital age: how trade, finance, people and data connect the world economy. Report, April. McKinsey Global Institute, San Francisco.

33. World Trade Organization. 2016. Report urges WTO members to resist protectionism and 'get trade moving again'. Reports on Trade Related Developments, WTO (http://bit.ly/2aniLun).

34. Hirschman (1945).

35. Hirschman himself is explaining the trade-based roots of Nazism and the warnings they give for post-war economic development.

36. See also Gellner (1983) and A. Giddens. 1985. *The Nation State and Violence: A Contemporary Critique of Historical Materialism*. Cambridge: Polity Press.

37. Q. Wright. 1994. Definitions of war. In *War* (edited by L. Freedman), chapter 24. Oxford University Press.

38. J. D. Singer and M. Small. 1994. International and Civil War data, 1861–1992. Correlates of War Project Series, Project ICPSR 9905.

39. S. Donnan and D. Sevastopulo. 2017. IMF warnings of US protectionism 'rubbish', says Ross. *Financial Times*, 16 April (http://on.ft.com/2y9abb1).

40. M. Wolf. 2017. Dealing with America's trade follies. *Financial Times*, 18 April (http://on.ft.com/2pe6fFH).

41. S. Roach. 2017. Donald Trump is suffering from trade deficit disorder. *Financial Times*, 7 March (http://on.ft.com/2xtoj1T).

42. B. Chu. 2017. What is Steve Bannon's 'economic nationalism'? And should we be scared? *The Independent*, 24 February (http://ind.pn/2lS2umX).

43. J. Cowley. 2017. The May Doctrine. *New Statesman*, 8 February (http://bit.ly/2llkztL).

44. J. Ganesh 2017. Forget Empire: Britain wants less of the world, not more. *Financial Times,* 10 April (http://on.ft.com/2omxnQU).

45. Fukuyama (1992).

46. Fukuyama (1992).

47. Kaldor (1999).

48. Kaldor (1999).

49. Kaldor (1999).

50. K. Ohmae. 1996. *The End of the Nation State: The Rise of Regional Economies – How New Engines of Prosperity Are Reshaping Global Markets.* London: Harper Collins.

51. J. Nye 1990. *Bound to Lead: The Changing Nature of American Power.* New York: Basic Books.

52. Baldwin (2016).

53. Baldwin (2016).

54. Hirschman (1945).

55. J. Breuilly. 2006. Introduction. In *Nations and Nationalism* (edited by E. Gellner), 2nd edition. Oxford: Basil Blackwell.

56. Goodhart (2017).

57. Emile Durkheim defined anomie as a 'condition in which society provides little moral guidance to individuals' in D. Lee and H. Newby. 1983. *The Problem of Sociology.* London: Unwin Hyman.

58. P. Dicken. 2007. *Global Shift: Mapping the Shifting Contours of the Global Economy.* London: Sage.

59. J. S. Nye Jr and W. Jizi. 2009. Hard decisions on soft power opportunities and difficulties for Chinese soft power. *Harvard International Review* Summer, 31(2).

60. B. Harris, S. Jung-a, S. Fei Ju and T. Hancock. 2017. China bans tour groups to South Korea as defence spat worsens. *Financial Times*, 3 March (http://on.ft.com/2lGkAoA).

61. von Clausewitz (2008).

62. From Dwight Eisenhower's Farewell Address to the Nation, 17 January 1961 (http://mcadams.posc.mu.edu/ike.htm).

63. D. A. Lake and R. Powell (eds). 1999. *Strategic Choice and International Relations*. Princeton University Press.

64. S. Cohen. 1972. *Folk Devils and Moral Panics*. London: MacGibbon and Kee Ltd. (Routledge Classics 2011 edition available online at Taylor & Francis e-Library: http://bit.ly/2xKLplA.)

65. Cohen (1972).

66. Dual-use export controls. See European Commission website: http://bit.ly/2c6DRKw.

67. Stockholm International Peace Research Institute. SIPRI Military Expenditure Database, 1949–2016 (http://bit.ly/2jWvdU2).

68. Asia Maritime Transparency Initiative and the Center for Strategic and International Studies. Eighteen maps that explain maritime security in Asia (http://bit.ly/2ykpj6d).

69. The change for South Africa in this figure is between 2008 and 2016 because of a lack of data for earlier years.

70. M. Brannermeier, H. James and J.-P. Landau. 2016. *The Euro and the Battle of Ideas*. Princeton University Press.

71. S. Green. 2016. *Reluctant Meister: How Germany's Past is Shaping Its European Future*. London: Haus.

72. Gellner (1983, 2006).

73. Fukuyama (1992).

74. Equant Analytics. 2016. Mind the £2.1 trillion dollar gap. Launch report (http://bit.ly/2f5KiBq).

75. T. Mitchell and X. Liu. 2017. China's trade with North Korea targeted by Trump. *Financial Times*, 23 April (http://on.ft.com/2pRCrLS).

76. UN International Trade Statistics Knowlegebase. 'Areas not elsewhere specified' (http://bit.ly/2xmO57T).

77. UN International Trade Statistics Knowlegebase.

78. J. Yazigi. 2014. Syria's war economy. European Council on Foreign Relations, Policy Brief, p. 3 (http://bit.ly/1elYQUC).

79. Uppsala Conflict Data Program. UCPD downloads (http://ucdp.uu.se/downloads/).

80. The data set includes deaths by terrorism that were based domestically and aimed at unsettling the existing regime.

81. The Fragile States Index (FSI) is published annually by the US-based Fund for Peace (www.fundforpeace.org/fsi/data/). The FSI highlights political, social and economic vulnerabilities versus a state's ability to deal with those vulnerabilities.

82. UN Office for Disarmament Affairs. Poorly managed ammunition: a key driver of conflict and crime (http://bit.ly/2wbtOTe).

83. P. Dörrie. 2015. The UN wants to regulate the arms trade: here's why it won't work. War is Boring, Medium.com, 24 February (http://bit.ly/1AILfno).

84. S. P. Huntingdon. 1997. *The Clash of Civilisations and the Remaking of World Order.* London: Simon and Shuster.

85. 'United we stand; divided we fall', open letter from Donald Tusk to the EU heads of state, 31 January 2017 (http://bit.ly/2kZfvLs).

86. M. Stone and M. Spetalnick. 2017. Exclusive: Trump administration prepares to ease export rules for US guns. *Reuters*, 19 September (http://reut.rs/2yghT3).

87. See F. Bermingham. 2017. Global export credit falls amid US Exim wipeout. *Global Change Review*, 12 July (http://bit.ly/2xAp7me); F. Bermingham. 2017. Banks signal the decline of traditional trade finance. *Global Change Review*, 5 July (http://bit.ly/2fjWYoG).

88. Asian Development Bank. 2016. Global trade finance gap reaches $1.6 trillion: SMEs hardest hit – ADB. News Release, 7 September (http://bit.ly/2wclToF).

89. R. Peston. 2012. HSBC to pay $1.9bn in US money laundering penalties. *BBC News*, 11 December (http://bbc.in/2cSGeXk).

90. J. Treanor. 2012. Standard Chartered to pay $340m fine to New York bank regulator. *The Guardian*, 14 August (http://bit.ly/2xjZfbh).

91. Data compiled from presentations at Trade Finance conferences during 2017 by Michael O'Kane and ANZ alongside own desk research.

92. International Chamber of Commerce. 2016. ICC Trade Register Report 2016 (http://bit.ly/2mEJ45d).

93. T. Phillips. 2017. China's Xi lays out $900bn Silk Road vision amid claims of empire-building. *The Guardian*, 14 May (http://bit.ly/2qeTtq3).